Why Bother?

Why do vote-suppression efforts sometimes fail? Why does police repression of demonstrators sometimes turn localized protests into massive, national movements? How do politicians and activists manipulate people's emotions to get them involved? The authors of *Why Bother?* offer a new theory of why people take part in collective action in politics and test it in the contexts of voting and protesting. They develop the idea that just as there are costs of participation in politics, there are also costs of abstention – intrinsic and psychological but no less real for that. That abstention can be psychically costly helps explain real-world patterns that are anomalies for existing theories, such as that sometimes increases in costs of participation are followed by more participation, not less. The book draws on a wealth of survey data, interviews, and experimental results from a range of countries, including the United States, Britain, Brazil, Sweden, and Turkey.

S. Erdem Aytaç is an assistant professor in the Department of International Relations at Koç University in Istanbul, Turkey. He received his Ph.D. in political science from Yale University in 2014. Aytaç's research interests lie in political behavior with a focus on democratic accountability and political participation. His previous work has appeared in the *Journal of Politics, Comparative Political Behavior, British Journal of Political Science, Political Behavior,* and the *Journal of Conflict Resolution,* among other journals. He is the recipient of the 2016 Young Scientist Award of Science Academy (Turkey) and the 2018 Sakıp Sabancı International Research Award.

Susan C. Stokes is the Tiffany and Margaret Blake Distinguished Service Professor of Political Science at the University of Chicago. She is a member of the American Academy of Arts and Sciences and past chair of the Yale Political Science Department. She is the author of *Mandates and Democracy: Neoliberalism by Surprise in Latin America* (Cambridge) and co-author of *Brokers, Voters, and Clientelism: The Puzzle of Distributive Politics* (Cambridge).

Cambridge Studies in Comparative Politics

General Editors

Kathleen Thelen *Massachusetts Institute of Technology*
Erik Wibbels *Duke University*

Associate Editors

Catherine Boone *London School of Economics*
Thad Dunning *University of California, Berkeley*
Anna Grzymala-Busse *Stanford University*
Torben Iversen *Harvard University*
Stathis Kalyvas *Yale University*
Margaret Levi *Stanford University*
Helen Milner *Princeton University*
Frances Rosenbluth *Yale University*
Susan Stokes *University of Chicago*
Tariq Thachil *Vanderbilt University*

Series Founder

Peter Lange *Duke University*

Other Books in the Series

Christopher Adolph, *Bankers, Bureaucrats, and Central Bank Politics: The Myth of Neutrality*
Michael Albertus, *Autocracy and Redistribution: The Politics of Land Reform*
Santiago Anria, *When Movements Become Parties: The Bolivian MAS in Comparative Perspective*
Ben W. Ansell, *From the Ballot to the Blackboard: The Redistributive Political Economy of Education*
Ben W. Ansell, David J. Samuels, *Inequality and Democratization: An Elite-Competition Approach*
Leonardo R. Arriola, *Multi-Ethnic Coalitions in Africa: Business Financing of Opposition Election Campaigns*
David Austen-Smith, Jeffry A. Frieden, Miriam A. Golden, Karl Ove Moene, and Adam Przeworski, eds., *Selected Works of Michael Wallerstein: The Political Economy of Inequality, Unions, and Social Democracy*
Andy Baker, *The Market and the Masses in Latin America: Policy Reform and Consumption in Liberalizing Economies*

Continued after the index

Why Bother?

Rethinking Participation in Elections and Protests

S. ERDEM AYTAÇ
Koç University

SUSAN C. STOKES
University of Chicago

CAMBRIDGE
UNIVERSITY PRESS

University Printing House, Cambridge CB2 8BS, United Kingdom

One Liberty Plaza, 20th Floor, New York, NY 10006, USA

477 Williamstown Road, Port Melbourne, VIC 3207, Australia

314–321, 3rd Floor, Plot 3, Splendor Forum, Jasola District Centre, New Delhi – 110025, India

79 Anson Road, #06–04/06, Singapore 079906

Cambridge University Press is part of the University of Cambridge.

It furthers the University's mission by disseminating knowledge in the pursuit of education, learning, and research at the highest international levels of excellence.

www.cambridge.org
Information on this title: www.cambridge.org/9781108475228
DOI: 10.1017/9781108690416

First published 2019

Printed in the United States of America by Sheridan Books, Inc.

A catalogue record for this publication is available from the British Library.

Library of Congress Cataloging-in-Publication Data
Names: Aytaç, S. Erdem, 1980– author. | Stokes, Susan Carol, author.
Title: Why bother? : rethinking participation in elections and protests /
    S. Erdem Aytaç, Koç University, Susan C. Stokes, University of Chicago.
Description: New York : Cambridge University Press, [2018] |
    Series: Cambridge studies in comparative politics |
    Includes bibliographical references and index.
Identifiers: LCCN 2018035529 | ISBN 9781108475228
Subjects: LCSH: Political participation. | Voter turnout. | Voting – Abstention. |
    Voting research. | Protest movements – Political aspects.
Classification: LCC JF799 .A93 2018 | DDC 323/.042–dc23
LC record available at https://lccn.loc.gov/2018035529

ISBN 978-1-108-47522-8 Hardback
ISBN 978-1-108-46594-6 Paperback

Erdem: For my family.
Susan: For Lewyn and Arlo, future participants.

Contents

Figures

Tables

Preface and Acknowledgments

When social scientists try to explain why people bother to take part in politics, they often fall back on a cost-benefit framework. If the benefits of going to the polls or into the streets outweigh the costs, people act; if the costs outweigh the benefits, they stay home. On the surface the formulation seems reasonable, if a little vague.

But the cost-benefit approach leads to several paradoxes and anomalies. One is the prediction, widely explored by scholars, that almost no one will vote in mass elections. Other anomalies have gone relatively unnoticed but are also troubling. The cost-benefit approach implies that people's participation decisions have little to do with how much they care about the outcome of the collective action in which they are considering taking part. One person thinks the sky will fall in if the wrong candidate wins or the protest fails; another sees nothing important at stake, whatever the outcome. By standard accounts, the first person is not more likely to take part than the second one.

Another implication of the cost-benefit approach is that escalations in the costs of participation should always be followed by reductions in the numbers of people taking part. In fact, it is not unusual for participation to remain unchanged or even grow in the wake of higher costs of participation. As we complete this book, two recent events remind us of this anomaly. In the opening days of 2018, protesters took to the streets in Mashhad, Iran's second largest city. The protests were met with predictable brutality. But the spike in costs of participation was followed not by a rapid containment of the protests; instead they spread to many other Iranian cities. This dynamic is not uncommon. We show in several settings that a surge in protests does not simply follow but is often caused by police brutality.

A few weeks earlier and half a world away, an event occurred that was perhaps as surprising as widespread protests in authoritarian Iran: a Democrat won a US Senate seat in the state of Alabama. One reason for his victory is that African-American voters turned out at high rates. Alabama is one of several southern states that have in recent years passed strict voter ID laws. The laws are widely viewed as efforts to suppress turnout among African-American voters. But in the 2017 Senate election, the turnout rate among registered black voters was higher than the rate among registered white voters.

Why did African-Americans in Alabama turn out to vote at high rates in an era when the costs of voting, in money, time, and trouble, had risen? According to some political scientists, the depressive effects of voter ID laws were countered by heavy voter mobilization – turnout was high *despite* voter ID laws.[1] There is undoubtedly a good deal of truth in this interpretation. But an activist involved in get-out-the-vote efforts in Alabama's black communities offered a different reason. LaTosha Brown saw the voter ID laws as having a mobilizing impact in themselves. "Historically and traditionally, there has been a strong voice of resistance to [measures] that are undemocratic." In other words, African-American turnout spiked not despite, but *because* of voter ID laws.

We wrote this book in search of a theory that turns these facts – which are anomalies in cost-benefit accounts – into predictions.

Many people helped us develop the ideas and carry out the research in this book. Our greatest debt is to our coauthors. Luis Schiumerini joined us in our study of social movements, and coauthored articles from which we draw in Chapters 5 and 6. Eli Rau worked with us on research into unemployment and turnout, which we draw on in Chapter 6. We are also indebted to our excellent research assistants. Melis Laebens and Gülay Türkmen-Dervişoğlu assisted us in our research into the Gezi Park uprising in Turkey. Leonid Peisakhin and Anastasia Rosovskaya undertook interviews in Kiev about Ukraine's Euromaidan protests. Simge Andı, Ezgi Elçi, Fatih Erol, and Firuze Simay Sezgin provided help with literature reviews and graphics in the book. Maria Tyrberg helped us navigate Swedish National Election Studies data, and Nedim Barut assisted with the implementation of our Istanbul survey in Chapter 6.

We are grateful for institutional support from Koç and Yale Universities. Zeynep Gürhan-Canlı, Dean of the College of Administrative Sciences and Economics of Koç, and Ian Shapiro, Director of Yale's MacMillan Center of International and Area Studies, provided support and encouragement, for which we are very grateful. The MacMillan Center is the home of the Yale Program on Democracy (YPD). In YPD workshops, we received invaluable advice from Kate Baldwin, Ana de la O, Germán Feierherd, Hélène Landemore, Adria Lawrence, Virginia Oliveros, David Rueda, Inga Saikkonen, Milan Svolik, and Tariq Thachil. We are also grateful to Steven Wilkinson, chair of Yale's Political Science Department, for his support and friendship. Sue Stokes spent a year at the Russell Sage Foundation, where her "fellow fellows" gave helpful

---

[1] Political scientist Eitan Hersh told the *New York Times*, "These laws are complicated to assess. Alabama was a place where there was a lot of campaigning, and when campaigns liven up, you have a lot of mobilization efforts." "Black Turnout in Alabama Complicates Debate on Voting Laws," December 24, 2017.

input. She is especially grateful to Elizabeth Cohen, Mona Lynch, Phil Cook, and Tom Palfrey, as well as to Sheldon Danziger, Suzanne Nichols, and the Foundation's staff.

We received terrific feedback from several other scholars: Mark Beissinger, Ali Çarkoğlu, Andy Eggers, Tim Feddersen, Miriam Golden, Greg Huber, Edgar Kaiser, Özge Kemahlıoğlu, Timur Kuran, Jodi LaPorte, Margaret Levi, Doug McAdam, Ezequiel Gonzalez Ocantos, Karl-Dieter Opp, Henrik Oscarsson, Shmulik Nili, Tom Palfrey, Steve Pincus, Hari Ramesh, Bryn Rosen-feld, David Rueda, Andy Sabl, Anastasia Shesterinina, Jazmin Sierra, Nick Valentino, and Elisabeth Wood. We would also like to acknowledge and thank the participants of seminars at Yale, the University of Essex, Sabancı University, Koç University, Princeton University, Northwestern University, New York University, the University of Maryland, Boğaziçi University, University of Rochester, Texas A&M University, Bahçeşehir University, Georgetown University, the University of Chicago, and University of Gothenburg.

Robert Dreesen, our editor at Cambridge University Press, encouraged us and managed the project through the review process with great efficiency and kindness. We are very grateful, as we are as well to two anonymous reviewers and to Kathleen Thelen and Erik Wibbels, editors of Comparative Politics series. We are also grateful to Jackie Grant and Robert Judkins at CUP and to Anya Hastwell for their assistance on the manuscript.

Erdem thanks his wife, Büke, for her love, encouragement, and especially for her patience as I spent several late nights on Skype to discuss the project with Sue. Our title comes from a suggestion offered by Jan King, at a dinner Sue enjoyed with Jan and Tony King and with Steve Pincus. Sue thanks Jan for her pithy phrase. We miss Tony.

Introduction: Rethinking Political Participation

It's hard to overstate what's at stake in popular participation in elections and protests. If turnout had been higher in parts of Michigan, Pennsylvania, and Wisconsin on November 8, 2016, Hillary Clinton might have become the 45th president of the United States. If turnout had edged up among young British voters on June 23, 2016, the United Kingdom might have decided to remain in the European Union. If a wave of protests had not taken off in Kiev in the winter of 2013–14, the government of Viktor Yanukovych might have remained in power instead of falling, as it did in February 2014. Russia would not have invaded Crimea and war would not have broken out in Eastern Ukraine. Changes in levels of popular participation can alter world history.

Yet the theories and ideas that social scientists – and, to a degree, campaigns and activists – rely on to explain why electoral turnout rises or falls, and why movements explode or fizzle, fall short. Some rely on assumptions that take little account of human psychology. Others fail to predict regularities that we observe the world around.

These shortcomings are well illustrated by the 2016 US presidential election and its aftermath. The campaign featured harsh language aimed at Muslims and at Mexican immigrants. In this period, many Muslim citizens who had not bothered to register to vote did so, and many Mexican immigrants initiated the process of becoming US citizens (Pogash 2016, Gonzalez-Barrera 2017). A natural explanation is that the harsh campaign rhetoric made members of these groups angry and fearful, and they saw the upcoming election as crucially important to them. For decades, "a lot of Muslims didn't see a lot of difference between the parties" explained a man at a registration drive in an Oakland, California mosque. A woman who had just picked up six voter-registration forms for herself and family members said, "This is the most important vote in our life" (Pogash 2016).

The day after Donald J. Trump's January 2017 presidential inauguration, the largest protest in US history took place. Between 3.2 and 5.2 million people took part in demonstrations in more than 650 cities across the country

(Chenoweth and Pressman 2017). Though billed as the Women's March, many men took part and, judging from the signs and slogans, what brought many to the streets was pent-up anger and disgust at the tone and content of the Trump campaign, and dismay at his victory.

Yet our prevailing social-science theories of political participation would reject these explanations for why people go to the polls and why they protest. The idea that people are driven to take part in collective action by their sense that much is at stake for them (or stay away when they see little at stake) cannot be easily accommodated by prevailing frameworks. What's more, fear, anger, and other emotions are mainly ignored. Leading theories struggle to make sense of the dynamics that seem so obviously at work in the mosque in Oakland or on the streets of Washington DC, New York, and other cities. Citizens who had earlier seen little difference between the parties and their programs had stayed away from the polls. They became more willing to vote when they began to see a real difference and to care much more about which candidate won and which lost. Protesters were angry at the incoming president and fearful about his administration's likely policies. They were therefore willing to bear the costs and risks of going into the streets.

In fact, from a theoretical standpoint, many social scientists find political participation puzzling, though the puzzlement is less widely shared by lay observers. We often find ourselves in awkward, even comical conversations with our friends, relatives, and students in which we explain to them why it is surprising that they vote and engage in other forms of mass participation. You should be puzzled, we patiently explain, by people's bothering to take part, given that their actions won't change the outcome and given that they will benefit (or suffer) equally, whether or not they participated. But don't worry, we hasten to add, we can explain this odd behavior! If they vote, perhaps they are expressing their partisan identification – but expressing it to whom, and what if they don't like political parties? Alternatively, they may be obeying a democratic norm that says it's their duty to take part. If they protest, perhaps they are part of a social network that values activism and shames the apathetic; yet what if images of the national flag do not appear in their mind's eye each Election Day, and what if they sometimes buck friends' subtle pressure to go to the rally, but at other times join in? Why do norms or the urge for political self-expression kick in, and why is social pressure effective, in some opportunities for collective action but not in others?

Well, the social scientist responds, maybe some elections or movements just don't seem important to them. But wait, the interlocutor counters, you just reminded me that my individual actions will not change the results. So I seem to have no concrete reason to take part, even if I care a lot.

Perhaps, then, the factor that shifts from election to election, and from small demonstrations to mass uprisings, are the obstacles in would-be participants' way: how hard it is to register to vote, or how likely a protester is to have an unhappy encounter with police batons and water cannons. These discouragements can be thought of as the *costs of participation*, and they certainly make a difference in participation rates. Varying costs of participation are often the social scientist's go-to explanation for why turnout goes up or down, or why a mass protest emerges from a small demonstration or fails to do so.

If the costs of participation were the whole story, however, we would never expect to see these costs rise and participation to go *up*.

If participation rose and fell with how costly it is – how much time, money, and planning it requires, and how much risk it entails – then legal barriers to voter participation should reliably depress turnout. But reality tells us otherwise. In the United States, laws aimed at making it more difficult for certain groups, such as African-Americans, to vote have certainly been effective over the decades. But research (reviewed in Chapter 2) shows that recent voter ID laws have been relatively ineffective. Though these laws discourage turnout, they also can be a mobilizing opportunity for leaders and energize the targeted groups.

In protests too, the costs of participation clearly rise when demonstrators encounter harsh police tactics: pepper spray and tear gas, rubber bullets, active batons. Yet, around the world, repression often has the opposite effect of the one intended. Harsh police tactics not infrequently turn small rallies into mass uprisings. Something more complex than the rise and fall of costs of participation seems to be going on.

The theory we develop in this book focuses on the interplay between the costs of participation and what we call *costs of abstention*. The former place burdens on people's pocketbooks and schedules. The latter place burdens on their psychic comfort and peace of mind. To focus on the former kinds of costs alone is to tell only half the story. Participation is determined by the net effect of the costs of participation *and* abstention.

Before delving into theories of participation, it's important to stress that our study also has practical implications. On voter turnout, in recent decades academics and campaigns have come together around a "get-out-the-vote" (GOTV) agenda – joint efforts to understand and increase participation in elections. One focus of this work has been on how best to *deliver* mobilizing messages to would-be voters in the most effective manner. This work teaches us, for instance, that marginal resources should be spent on face-to-face canvassing over robocalls. We have also learned, with field experiments, about how social pressure can be deployed to get people to the polls. This work casts a powerful light on one emotional motivator: shame.

Much less work by GOTV investigators has focused on the *content* of the messages delivered to would-be participants, though obviously campaigns have long found focus groups and other message-testing techniques to be of great value. What we shall see is that the last type of effort is by no means in vain. The message matters; and, as we shall demonstrate in this book, it matters not least for its work in eliciting emotional responses that draw people to collective action. These emotional responses go well beyond shame and include anger and moral outrage, enthusiasm, and, in some settings, anxiety.

Likewise, getting the theory right on protest participation has practical import. One example has to do with the effects of violence at protests, whether carried out by the police and authorities, or by movement participants. To the extent that both sides are concerned about broader public opinion, they will be helped by the perception that any violence which takes place has been committed by the other side, while they remain peaceful.[1] A disciplined passivity, while the other sides engages in harsh tactics, will garner not only more external support but may also draw in large numbers of participants. In the United States, early in the Trump administration, conservatives in several state legislatures proposed to shield drivers who might injure protesters from legal sanctions, if the protesters were demonstrating on roads or highways. Our study indicates that such laws would be counterproductive from the standpoint of their proponents: they are as likely to build support for protests as they are to scare demonstrators away.

LIMITATIONS OF CURRENT THEORIES

The limitations of theories of mass political participation have not kept social scientists from collecting data and crafting sophisticated accounts of the kinds of people who take part and those who do not, or from *explaining* participation, in the sense of making accurate predictions about who will take part in what kind of action. But like physical scientists observing bodies fall to the ground before the Newtonian revolution, our lack of adequate theories makes a deeper understanding elusive, and leads to questionable interpretations of the observations we make.

A leading but problematic interpretation is that mass participation is well-explained by rational choice theory. With regard to voting, the problem is on display in two important empirical studies on turnout in the United States, published roughly 20 years apart: Steven Rosenstone and John Mark Hansen's *Mobilization, Participation, and Democracy in America* (1993), and Jan Leighley and Jonathan Nagler's *Who Votes Now?* (2014). Both pairs of authors tried, not entirely successfully in our view, to press their findings into the box of rational choice. Rosenstone and Hansen noted that people lack individual incentives to vote or to seek out information relevant to politics, burdensome tasks that can be left to others. They wrote that "Left to their own devices …the public's involvement in the political process would be defeated by two difficult problems: the paradoxes of participation and rational ignorance" (2003[1993]: 6). These obstacles are overcome, they argued, by political parties and campaigns, which rationally make an effort to get people to the polls. So the motivation to participate is extrinsic to the individual – he or she will not do so unless prodded by campaigns or political parties. By extension, demonstrators would not take to the streets without the prodding of activists.

---

[1] As explained in Chapter 4, this idea has been addressed in the context of the US civil rights movement by Denis Chong (1991).

Two decades later, Leighley and Nagler (2014: 122) espoused "a cost and benefit framework of voter turnout." An important finding they report is that "an individual will be more likely to vote when candidates take policy positions providing the voter with more distinct choices" (p. 124). Their words evoke the Muslim-American citizen who suddenly sees a world of difference between Democratic and Republican candidates, where earlier they looked like Tweedle Dum and Tweedle Dee. But there is a tension in Leighley and Nagler's invocation of the difference in candidates' policy position as a prod for getting citizens to the polls. Cost-benefit accounts discount such differences. The reason, again, is that however enormous the gap in benefits to an individual of her preferred candidate's winning, her ballot will not make her preferred result more likely to any perceptible degree. Therefore Leighley and Nagler have to do some work to squeeze the polarized-policy effect on turnout into the box of costs and benefits.

They turn to a seminal theoretical paper by John Aldrich (1993), who pointed out that the costs of voting are usually very small and campaigns can easily overcome them. When candidates offer sharply different programs, Leighley and Nagler also reason, parties invest more resources in getting people to the polls. So again we have people responding entirely to extrinsic pressures to participate. Why they respond to these extra efforts by parties is unclear; within the tenets of rational choice theory, they should not. The Aldrich–Leighley–Nagler approach, like Rosenstone and Hansen's, falls back on *costs* of participation, even though their findings point to the perceived *benefits* that people anticipate gaining if their favored candidate prevails as a key factor driving them to the polls.

Social scientists who have crafted general explanations of why people protest have been less troubled by classic problems of collective action. But their accounts, too, have tended to fall short of a model that simultaneously incorporates a sense of the material costs and risks that protesters face, as well as the social, psychological, and moral compulsions that can turn bystanders into participants. There is much to be gained, we hope to persuade the reader, from a general framework for explaining participation that can be modified to make sense of people's decision to vote or abstain and their decisions to protest or stay at home.

WHY STUDY VOTING AND PROTESTING TOGETHER?

Why people turn out to vote and why they join protests are questions that are usually studied separately. Political scientists examine electoral participation; sociologists and social psychologists, movement participation. Whatever the reasons for this scholarly division of labor, it has not arisen because the choices that would-be participants make are vastly different in the two settings. Whether the choice is to vote or to demonstrate, financial and time constraints can get in the way. Both, what's more, involve cognitive effort: a person has to figure out what protesters are calling for and whether she agrees with their goals, or which candidate is honest or proposes policies that she supports. The outcomes both of elections and of protests are public goods, so people may well ask themselves about both activities, *Why bother?*

To be clear, there are differences between voting and protesting. As we explain in later chapters, the costs involved in protesting tend to be greater – on average, joining demonstrations is more demanding in time and presents greater risks than voting. People may feel a sense of duty to participate in both settings, but duty *to whom* differs – to society at large for voters, to friends, acquaintances, and fellow-travelers for protesters. In both cases, would-be participants are sensitive to the strategic context in making their choices. But these strategic contexts are different. For instance, anticipation that an election will be close may move voters to the polls, whereas people may be moved to join protests the larger they expect the crowds on the streets to be – in this case, the greater the number of participants, the better.

The key point is that would-be voters and would-be protesters take the same factors into consideration when they decide whether to participate or stay home, though the factors will weigh differently in their decisions. More technically, the basic parameters are the same, even if their values will typically be different, and even if they interact in distinct ways.

By placing these two crucial instruments of popular participation in the same framework, we call attention to an underlying unity across disparate spheres of political action. People are drawn to the polling place or the rally when they see the outcome as important – notwithstanding that the outcomes are public goods. They may be driven to act by emotional responses to elite actions; we will show that one key emotion, anger, is a powerful propellent to collective action, whether that action is to vote or to demonstrate. Would-be participants in both kinds of action may be sensitive to a sense of moral obligations to act; however, we will show that these moral obligations are more situational than absolute.

Democratic theorists place quite different values on these two forms of popular action. Once we have developed and tested a theory that, in modified form, accounts for both, at the end of the book we touch on the value of elections and protests as instruments of democracy. Where many theorists of democracy place elections at the center and protests at the periphery – or beyond the pale – we find them to be complementary, each one making up for the shortcomings of the other as instruments of accountability, representation, and political equality.

In this book, we do not merely assert that similar factors influence people's decisions about whether to participate in these two distinct venues of collective action. We treat the assertions as testable propositions and subject them to testing. We do so with novel data of diverse kinds – sample surveys, survey experiments, in-depth interviews, and field observation – and gathered from disparate locations – the United States, Great Britain, Sweden, Brazil, Turkey, and Ukraine. Cutting-edge techniques allow us to disentangle knotty questions. To give a few examples, it has widely been shown that important (e.g., presidential, national) elections elicit higher turnout than less-important (e.g., local) ones. Is the explanation simply that candidates for high office work harder, their parties pouring more resources into mobilizing voters, when the stakes are high? Could it also be the case that voters are sensitive to the importance of the post to be filled, independent of elite efforts to mobilize them? With observational data it is hard to adjudicate between the two explanations. The experimental techniques that we deploy allow us to show that intrinsic forces induce people to participate in important elections, even when they are not mobilized by elites.

In turn, social movement theorists have appropriately criticized "grievance" models of protest, which posit that features of the social environment (say, inequality) create grievances and the aggrieved are at heightened risk of collective action. It has been pointed out that scholars in this mold have failed to measure grievance levels among those who demonstrate and those who stay home. To overcome this problem, we carry out sample surveys in key cities where major protests have taken place. Doing so allows us to compare participants with nonparticipants. Likewise, cascade models of social movements rest on the intuition that many people will join a rally when they anticipate that it will be large but stay home when they anticipate that it will be small. Yet, surprisingly little systematic evidence has been gathered to confirm this suspicion; we gather just such data. We also delve more deeply into what lies behind protest cascades.

WHAT WOULD A GOOD THEORY DO?

If received theories fail to make sense of people's decisions to take part in collective civic action, what would a satisfactory theory accomplish? It would do two things. First, it would rely on *basic assumptions* that make sense, ones that accord with the findings of experts and the intuitions of lay citizens. Second, it would produce *accurate predictions*, ones that make sense of observed facts about participation – who does and who does not take part, and why participation swells under some circumstances and ebbs under others.

In our effort to construct such a theory, we are by no means starting from scratch. Indeed, the allusion to the Newtonian revolution in a previous paragraph is misleading. Much existing theory does not rely on fundamental errors, equivalent to the belief that the universe revolves around the Earth. Instead, in writing this book we have drawn on a wealth of insightful but incomplete (and, at moments, ill-considered) theorizing. The party-mobilization theory, alluded to a moment ago, is a case in point. No one would deny that parties and campaigns work hard to get out the vote, but we need to look more closely at what they do to achieve this end and why it works. We will argue in Chapter 6 that one thing they do is offer causal interpretations of adverse circumstances that voters face, interpretations that elicit citizens' anger and move them to the polls. So mobilization models are not so much incorrect as incomplete; they place the sun at the center of the galaxy but have not fully fleshed out the nature of the gravitational pull.

What is needed, then, is not so much a paradigm shift as a paradigm realignment. As Chapter 2 makes clear, beginning a half century ago, economic approaches to democracy became deeply influential in shaping our understanding of mass political participation. In some respects these influences sent us, collectively, in the wrong direction, obscuring important insights into the psychological and social bases of collective action. Theorists who tried to press participation into a narrow mold of individual cost-benefit calculations came up empty-handed, failing to make sense of a most basic fact about democracy, viz: that rational individuals do vote in mass elections, just as they do take part in protests, even – in the latter case – at risk of bodily injury. But the economic approach was not unproductive. It eventually spawned models which, though still failing to fulfill the criterion of sensible assumptions, came closer to success than previous efforts. What's more, though economic theorists remained insensitive to the emotional substrate of mass action, their insistence that participation imposes costs on those who act, and that these costs, too, must be part of the equation, was an important lesson not to be forgotten. In Chapter 2 we review theories of electoral participation and offer our own alternative, which, we hope, employs realistic assumptions and makes sense of observed patterns. In Chapter 4 we modify this model so that it can yield insights into protest participation.

Three general points are worth making about our model in advance:

(1) **Abstention can be costly**. Received theory, as we have just noted, emphasizes the costs of participation as a factor that, on its own, works against people taking part in voting, protesting, and other forms of collective political action. But this view is one-sided. Just as there are costs of participation, so there are also costs of abstention. The former are material and cognitive, the latter intrinsic and psychological, but no less real for that.

That abstention can be intrinsically costly helps explain why people sometimes bear very high costs to be able to participate; and they do so, typically, because they care a lot about the outcome. Referendums that pose basic questions about rights, sovereignty, and identities often see very high rates of participation (LeDuc 2015). The 2016 British referendum on EU membership drew close to 34 million people to the polls: 72% of the electorate, compared to the 66% who voted in the previous general election in 2015. The 2014 referendum on Scottish independence drew 85% of eligible voters to the polls. This turnout rate was 20 percentage points higher than the average in Scotland in the prior four British national elections.[2]

---

[2] Qvortrup (2013) and Butler and Ranney (1994) find that turnout in referendums varies more than in general elections. According to Butler and Ranney, turnout is lower, on average, in referendums than in candidate elections, but the standard deviation is higher – a subset of referendums, like those cited here, drive participation up to unusually higher levels.

People sometimes bear heavy costs to take part in collective action. Protesters in democracies new and old can face police clubs, tear gas, jail, and worse. Voting is usually not dangerous, but it can be costly. Ireland held a referendum on same-sex marriage in 2015. Irish citizens living in the UK traveled by sea and air to vote in it. Airline tickets between London and Dublin sold out on the day of the vote (Hakim and Dalby 2015). Why would people pay so much money and go to so much trouble to cast a ballot? Hannah Little, an Irish woman living in London who flew back to vote, explained,

"With Irish pals, every time we meet up, going home for the referendum has been at the forefront ... My plan is to go home to settle and have children. If my kids turn out to be gay, I want my voice to be heard now" (McDonald 2015).

Did Hannah Little not realize that her vote was extremely unlikely to be the decisive one in favor of same-sex marriage in Ireland? Did she not realize that if she moved back to Ireland and had gay offspring, they would be able to legally marry same-sex partners whether or not their mother had troubled herself to make the pilgrimage back for the 2015 referendum? We present evidence in the pages to come that the answer to both questions, for her and for many people like her, is "yes," they do understand these facts. They take part when they care a lot because *not* participating would be to enter into a state of dissonance: these are costs of abstention.

We are certainly not the first to notice these latter kinds of costs. Rational choice theory dug itself out of the "paradox of voting" – its prediction of near-zero turnout in large electorates – by adducing a *duty* to vote. People who feel this duty would forgo the payoffs derived from fulfilling it, were they to abstain. But the construct of duty does not solve every problem. Conceptualized as an encouragement to vote, it is static and does not explain the ups and downs in levels of turnout across elections. Nor does it explain why common people take part in collective political action for which there is no generally recognized duty to take part, such as in street protests. Network and shaming models, where a person runs the risk of being shunned if he or she stays home, also imply that abstention is costly. But these models focus excessively on the role of one's immediate personal networks in driving political participation. They struggle – as duty models do – to explain why particular kinds of elections predictably spark widespread participation, whereas in others, popular involvement is anemic.

A key move we make, then, is to posit costs of abstention: straight-up disutility from not taking part, the magnitude of which depends, *inter alia*, on how much a person sees as at stake in the outcome.

(2) **Many people think about the strategic setting of elections and protests from a supraindividual point of view.** To unlock the mysteries of political participation, just as important as the particular factors that influence whether a person will take part is the vantage point from which people approach the decision.

Prior theorists, for understandable reasons of parsimony and elegance, have stuck to one level at once, usually that of the individual, who is seen as thinking about the costs and benefits of action entirely as they influence him or her, individually. Others have posited that people think about what to do from the vantage point of a social planner or party leader; citizens are thought to consider both benefits and costs at this macro level. Our theory of costly abstention posits that people are capable of thinking at distinct levels. They consider the costs of participation from the vantage point of their own time and effort. They consider the strategic context – the probabilities of the movement succeeding, the favored candidate winning – from a vantage point above the individual, typically of a candidate or party or movement leader. Regarding the *benefits* of alternative outcomes, they regard these at both individual and higher levels. What our multilevel theory gives up in parsimony, it gains in accuracy.

(3) **To understand political participation, we need less economics, more psychology.** Political scientists are well aware of the ways in which cognitive distortions and biases influence the perceptions and choices of citizens (and of political elites). We are becoming increasingly aware that emotions also influence our political perceptions and actions. A new appreciation has emerged in the social sciences of emotions and cognition as not in tension with one another, but working in concert. The recent psychological turn, advanced in no small measure by behavioral economists, has nurtured the field of political psychology, and in some measure we will be advocating a return to social-psychological ideas about participation which many scholars set aside with the rise of rational choice.

We take rational choice theory seriously and have used it heavily in our own work. But our desire to understand collective action has drawn us toward psychology. An initial intuition, as we began our research, was that when people care about who their elected leaders will be and what courses their communities and countries will take, they may find themselves drawn to collective action. They will vote and perhaps even demonstrate, even without anyone telling them they should, sometimes without having to think very hard about their decisions to participate. Not just social shame or moral reflection but also something much quicker and more spontaneous often spurs people to act.

Some of our intuitions come from introspection. We consider what it would feel like to care a lot about the outcome of an election but to stay home and let others decide. We imagine this as an uncomfortable state of dissonance. We soon found our intuitions echoed in the words of people we interviewed. For instance, a man in Kiev told our interviewers about the events that drew him to activism in 2013, in what would become the Euromaidan protests. He remembered how he felt when he saw the image of a young woman who had been beaten at a rally: "You know, there are sometimes moments when you feel like you are coming apart because it is no longer possible to tolerate the situation."

We groped, initially, with phrases like "internal dissonance"; later we learned much more, from social and political psychology, about preconscious responses, approach emotions, and the tricky, sometimes surprising effects of anger, moral outrage, anxiety, and guilt. Though we have by no means become political psychologists, we have certainly leaned heavily upon political psychology to help us make sense of the world of popular participation.

A MAP OF THE BOOK

What comes next? Chapters 2 and 3 focus on voting. The first task we undertake in Chapter 2 is to demonstrate the achievements, but also the shortcomings, of inherited theories of electoral participation. The range and inventiveness of the accumulated theory make an extensive review necessary. Our second task in the chapter is to offer our own theory, which places intrinsic costs of abstention at the center.

Chapter 3 tests our theory against others. We find support for the construct of intrinsic costs of abstention, alluded to here and discussed more fully in Chapter 2. Costs of abstention do indeed influence people's willingness to vote and clearly rise and fall with how much people see as at stake in the outcome. We also test propositions about close elections making people more willing to vote – even when they are not prodded to do so by campaigns or parties – and about the power of a sense of civic duty to get people to the polls. We show that civic duty makes a difference; but we find it to be more of a conditional than an absolute norm, so that when it is an internalized norm, it is like other costs of abstention.

Chapters 4 and 5 focus on protests. Chapter 4 asks, *What explains why people join protests?* We begin with a review of the rich theoretical literature to provide some explanations, and then present a costly abstention theory of participation, modified in ways that make it relevant to protests. In Chapter 5 we draw on original research in several developing democracies, as well as extensive secondary literature on protests in many regions of the world, to test key propositions derived from our model. We probe whether the goals of protests matter and to what kinds of people; whether bystanders' expectations about the size of protests influence their decisions to take part; and show that police repression can indeed make protests grow. This last issue can appear paradoxical if one does not take into account that repression can drive up the costs of abstention at the same time that it drives up the costs of participation.

Chapter 6 demonstrates the importance of taking emotional responses into account when explaining the ebbs and flows of both forms of popular participation. In particular, it is hard to make sense of the dynamics of participation while ignoring the role of anger and moral outrage. We demonstrate the power of emotions in several countries. Scholars have tried to explain unemployed Americans' drop in turnout rates (and, in some settings, revival of these rates over time) with reference to the opportunity costs that they bear when they go to the polls. Their behavior is better explained, we demonstrate, by taking into account the emotions they experience, emotions which strategic politicians sometimes choose to stir up. Outside of the United States, the key role of emotions in mobilizing people comes through in nationally representative surveys in Britain and Sweden, which we also analyze. In turn, when the police in Turkey attack demonstrators and protests surge, the explanation is not that Turkish citizens' support for the government has dropped or that they are newly confident in the potential for success of the protests. Instead, we demonstrate how anger and moral outrage turn bystanders into participants. Hence, approach emotions like anger are key to simulating collective action, both at the polling place and in the streets.

In Chapter 7 we reprise the costly abstention theory and its predictions, our methods for testing it, and the empirical support that we have adduced for it. We also anticipate objections to the theory and respond to them. Next, we assess the payoffs from thinking side-by-side about voting and protesting. We consider what our theory of turnout implies for theories of vote choice once people are inside the voting booth. We also pose the question, *What is the appropriate normative status of these two key tools of popular participation?*

A word, finally, on the geographic sources of our data and research. The theories we test are fairly general, the scope conditions broad. The theory of electoral participation is relevant to democracies in general, though the relevance will be less in some cases, such as places in which voting is compulsory or where vote buying is common. We test propositions about voting mainly with survey experiments of US voters, though we also work with survey data from other countries. Our focus on US respondents is purely a convenience, reflecting the availability of online samples for recruitment into survey experiments.[3] Likewise, the theory of protest mobilization is general to democracies, though we incorporate insights from protests in authoritarian regimes (such as in the Arab Spring countries). As explained in Chapter 4, the role of political violence is aptly demonstrated in new democracies.

---

[3] We make use of Amazon.com's Mechanical Turk (www.mturk.com) and Survey Sampling International (www.surveysampling.com) online samples, as indicated. In Aytaç's (Turkey) and Stokes's (Latin America) regions of special expertise, compulsory voting is widespread. Compulsory voting (especially with real sanctions) drives up participation and makes it less variable (see the review in Blais 2006). Therefore we pay less attention to these regions on the elections side of the study, though they offer important evidence on the protest side. Outside of the United States, on voting, the British Election Study and the Swedish National Election Studies have included verified measures of turnout, confirming their respondents' participation or abstention from constituency records, making them valuable sources, since most others use self-reported voting.

2

Theories of Voter Participation: A Review and a New Approach

Theories of electoral participation are legion, but none is fully persuasive. A persuasive theory must be built on reasonable assumptions and make sense of observed facts. Some basic ones are these: rational people vote; the importance people place on the outcome of an election influences their participation decisions; turnout is often high in close races; and spikes in the costs of participation do not always reduce turnout – in some instances they may increase it. We begin this chapter by reviewing the theoretical literature on turnout. Next we lay out an original, costly abstention theory of electoral participation that predicts observed patterns and rests on intuitive assumptions.

A REVIEW OF THEORIES OF TURNOUT

Early social-psychological models. Early work in political behavior attributed people's willingness to go to the polls to psychological factors, which in turn were shaped by a person's family socialization, schooling, and by their organizational experiences in adulthood. A study that remains influential is *The American Voter* (1960). Its authors described "motivational forces" and "psychological influences that affect the likelihood that an individual will vote" (p. 90). Engagement with politics, interest in campaigns, and strength of partisan ties were predictive of turnout behavior. Among *The American Voter*'s samples, those who agreed strongly that voting is a duty were very likely to vote, although some who expressed only lukewarm agreement also voted. Some people who did not vote were kept from doing so by legal barriers (e.g., they had moved and had not registered in their new communities) or by practical obstacles (e.g., they were stuck at work from before the polls opened until after they closed). A sense of personal efficacy – more widespread among the highly educated than among those with little education – was predictive of participation, as were interest in the campaign and the perception that the election

13

outcome was important. The perceived closeness of the race also mattered, but only among people who cared about the outcome: "the turnout behavior of a person of weak preference is not affected by whether he thinks the election will be close" (1960: 100).[1]

This pioneering work in political behavior eschewed abstract theorizing, but it did put forth generalizations about turnout (and vote choice). Certain psychological traits and life experiences increased people's sense of efficacy and attentiveness to politics, and hence their propensity to participate. These general conclusions rested on the correlates of voting that Campbell and his coauthors uncovered, correlates that would reappear in study after study of American politics in the decades that followed.[2] Education encourages participation, in large part because it cultivates interest in politics and a sense of personal efficacy.[3] Education explains more variation in participation than does income, but high-income individuals are more likely to vote than low-income ones. Middle-aged people are more likely to vote than the young, and voting tends to become habitual. All of these factors reappear in studies of political participation in the United States from the 1970s (e.g., Wolfinger and Rosenstone 1980), the 1980s and 1990s (e.g., Rosenstone and Hansen 1993, Verba et al. 1995), and right through the second decade of the twenty-first century (e.g., Leighley and Nagler 2014).

Studies of Western European voters uncovered many of the same correlates of voting as in the United States. We analyze turnout in Britain and Sweden, two countries in which national election surveys verify the turnout behavior of their respondents. Since the survey researchers checked whether each respondent had voted or abstained against the election rolls, these surveys avoid problems of social desirability bias (people reporting they turned out when in fact they did not), and get us closer to the behavior of interest. We study the 2010 general elections in Britain with data from the British Election Study (BES; Whiteley and Sanders 2014) and in Sweden with data from the Swedish National Election Studies Program (SNES; Holmberg and Oscarsson 2017). The dependent variables in Table 2.1 are verified turnout. The correlates have much in common with those identified for the United States of the 1950s by Campbell and his coauthors. Older individuals, those with high incomes and more education, married people, union members, nonminorities in Britain and

---

[1] The Electoral College seemed not to enter into the calculus of American voters in the 1950s: respondents indicated that the closeness of a presidential race nationally, and not in their states, had "cognitive and motivational significance" (Campbell 1960: 100).

[2] With the exception of sex: in the 1950s, women's participation lagged behind that of men, especially in the South (Campbell 1960: 485–93).

[3] Though most observational (e.g., Rosenstone and Hansen 1993, Verba et al. 1995) and some experimental (Sondheimer and Green 2010) research supports the link between education and participation, this is not universally true. Berinsky and Lenz (2011) find that an exogenous increase in educational attainment had no significant effect on turnout. They speculate that people with higher cognitive skills are prone both to stay in school and to turn out in elections.

TABLE 2.1 *Correlates of turnout in Britain and Sweden – BES and SNES 2010*

Dep. var.: verified turnout	Britain		Sweden	
	Coefficient	SE	Coefficient	SE
Female	0.12	(0.14)	0.43*	(0.20)
Age	0.03**	(0.005)	0.17**	(0.06)
Married	0.36*	(0.14)	0.91**	(0.24)
Education	0.16**	(0.06)	0.15**	(0.03)
Income	0.07**	(0.02)	0.24*	(0.09)
Union Member	0.47*	(0.19)	−0.05	(0.21)
Minority	−0.58*	(0.23)		
Foreign-born			−1.03**	(0.28)
Civic Duty	0.41**	(0.06)		
Constant	−3.28**	(0.38)	0.02	(0.38)
Observations	1,490		2,019	

Note: Logistic regressions with standard errors in parentheses. $*p < 0.05$, $**p < 0.01$.
Source: Whiteley and Sanders (2014) and Holmberg and Oscarsson (2017).

native-born citizens in Sweden, and those feeling a civic duty have turned out at elevated rates in these recent elections.[4]

Comparative studies of turnout outside of the United States and Western Europe, where individual survey data were scarce, have tended to focus on institutional factors. Investigators have asked, for instance, whether proportional or majoritarian electoral rules encouraged higher rates of participation, and whether people vote at higher rates in systems with unicameral or with bicameral legislatures.[5] The logic behind these expected institutional effects, as emphasized by Franklin (2004) and others, is that people care more about important elections and therefore are more willing to vote in them. Though the link identified by these scholars between voters' perceptions of the importance of the election and turnout may seem entirely intuitive, it is severed in rational choice models, as we shall see. None of these earlier scholars sees the logic as vitiated by problems of collective action.

Social-psychological approaches to turnout, in the tradition of *The American Voter*, continue to be a source of important findings and insights into

[4] In the Swedish Election Study there were no questions related to the minority status and civic duty perceptions of respondents. Note that unlike in Britain, being a member of a trade union (or professional staff association) is not a positive predictor of turnout in Sweden. This might be related to the much higher unionization rate in Sweden; 54% of respondents in the Swedish survey report being union members, compared with 19% of the British sample.

[5] For a review, see Blais (2006). Another line of research, pursued both at aggregate and at individual levels, explores the impact of the economy on turnout; see Arcelus and Meltzer (1975), Fiorina (1978), Powell (1982), Rosenstone (1982), Jackman (1987), Franklin (2004), Burden and Wichowsky (2014), and Kasara and Suryanarayan (2015).

participation. In recent years the political-psychology agenda has shifted from explaining the socializing role of family and institutions to tracing the impact of cognitive biases, emotions, and adaptive or reinforcement learning on people's preference formation and propensity to act.[6] Political psychologists have shown that cognitive structures of memory and association impinge on political preference formation.[7] Emotions also influence political behavior. Appraisal theory demonstrates that people attribute causal responsibility to actors or forces for events that influence their welfare; their emotional reactions follow from these appraisals (Valentino et al. 2011; for a review, see Brader and Marcus 2013).

To make the assumptions and comparisons across the theories presented here more concrete, we introduce a hypothetical voter, whom we call George. Early social-psychological accounts would have anticipated that George would be a marginal voter – one who is usually on the fence between turning out and staying home – if his educational level was not high (for instance, if his education ended after high school). If he were lower-middle or working class, his income level would also have predicted relatively lower turnout, an effect interpreted by these scholars as driven by relatively less engagement in politics. Yet they would have stressed his greater likelihood of voting if his parents had been strong partisans; they would have communicated these commitments to him, as well as the habit of voting, both of which would have represented countervailing effects of low levels of income and education. More recent political-psychological theories would have been interested as well in the ways in which any partisan orientation shaped George's political perceptions and levels of engagement, as well as the emotional impact of adversity that he might face, as a working-class American.

The individual correlates of voting discerned by early scholarship changed little in the decades after the appearance of *The American Voter*. But the theoretical interpretation of them shifted sharply. The early, social-psychologically inflected literature assumed that the costs of voting might erode participation. But it did not see voting as potentially hampered by a collective action problem – by the tendency to leave costly participation to someone else.

The turn to economic models of voting. *The American Voter*, published in 1960, was to become a classic title in political behavior, built on social-psychological foundations. *An Economic Theory of Democracy* by Anthony Downs, published three years earlier, was to become a classic in political behavior and party competition, built on economic foundations. The decision of whether to vote or abstain was less central to Downs's concerns than was the choice of which party to support (and parties' choices of what policy positions

---

[6] On reinforcement learning and habitual voting, see, among others, Kanazawa (1998), Bendor et al. (2003), Gerber et al. (2003), and Fowler (2006).

[7] As in "schema theory"; see e.g., Conover and Feldman (1984), Huber et al. (2012); for critical reviews, see Kuklinski et al. (1991), and Bullock et al. (2015).

to take). Downs proposed that voters' candidate decision-rule was: *choose the one that offers me the greatest utility benefits*. In practice this meant supporting the incumbent if the utility income gained on his watch was greater than the utility income one would reasonably have expected to gain under a government of the opposition.

Downs noticed, somewhat in passing, that the difference-in-utility-income decision-rule implied a very significant anomaly: the act of casting a ballot in a mass election would virtually never increase a voter's utility income. This is true for the reasons already mentioned: a single person's vote will basically never make the difference between her favored candidate winning or losing. What's more, she will receive whatever benefits are to be had from a government's term in office, whether she voted in the election that brought it to power or abstained. So the benefits side of the cost-benefit calculation is zero. Voting is costly, even if the costs are small. Therefore, rational people will not vote.

The anomaly that Downs pointed to would absorb scholarly energies for many years, right up to the present. The facts underlying the *paradox of voting* are real: it is in the nature of things that voting is costly; single votes basically never do change the outcome – who wins and who loses; and many of the goods (and bads) that governments produce are public: jointly produced and nonrival in consumption.[8] But these facts only add up to an obstacle to voting if people go to the polls with the mindset of securing a private benefit for themselves. They might instead be driven to the polls by the psychic dissonance entailed in caring about an outcome and failing to act. Alternatively, they might be driven by social pressures. What's more, citizens might assess the strategic context of the election, not from the vantage point of themselves but of party leaders or campaigns. If so, they will not necessarily be kept home by collective action problems.

As the next half century would show, theories that hewed close to Downs's original formulation predict zero, or close to zero, turnout. The logic was clearly fleshed out in one of the most influential papers ever published in political science, William Riker and Peter Ordeshook's "A Theory of the Calculus of Voting" (1968). Their simple mathematical formalization of the individual's rewards from voting helped clarify the nature of the problem.

Riker and Ordeshook related the *rewards* of voting (R) to the differential *benefits* of the outcome (B), the *probability* of an individual's vote being pivotal (p), and the *cost* of voting (C), as laid out in the following equation:

$$R = (p)B - C. \tag{2.1}$$

The model predicts that a rational (and numerate) person will not vote. For the rewards of voting to be positive, the differential benefit (B) he receives

---

[8] Though some are also private goods, such as public-sector employment, or club goods, such as economic development schemes that benefit some regions but not others.

"from the success of his more preferred candidate over his less preferred one," multiplied by the probability (p) of his vote being pivotal (breaking a tie), must outweigh the cost (C) he incurs from voting. But in an electorate that has more than one hundred members, p is exceedingly small, indeed basically indistinguishable from zero. Therefore, the product (p)B also basically equals zero; since voting is costly, people will abstain.

To get them back to the polls, Riker and Ordeshook introduced an innovation that harkened back to *The American Voter*. Recall that many people sampled by Campbell, Converse, Miller, and Stokes believed that citizens have a duty to vote; those who felt this duty strongly were more likely to turn out than those who felt it weakly or not at all. Riker and Ordeshook used the letter D to represent a duty to participate:[9]

$$R = (p)B - C + D \qquad\qquad (2.2)$$

The D term brings Riker and Ordeshook's model in line with one key fact about elections: people vote. It does *not* bring it in line with several other key facts. One is that turnout propensities rise and fall with the perceived importance of the result – its "utility differential" for individuals. In Chapter 3, we will offer ample evidence that utility differentials are key to people's decisions about whether to go to the polls. In Riker and Ordeshook's framework, B remains orphaned by a p that is indistinguishable from zero.

Riker and Ordeshook's reliance on a normative factor, D, to explain turnout rankled economically oriented theorists and invited mocking commentary from those critical of rational choice theory (e.g., Barry 1970, Green and Shapiro 1994). Perhaps for these reasons, rational choice theorists kept working on models that would stay closer to Downs's original formulation but would predict positive (and, preferably, widespread) participation. They were not especially successful.

The next move was to "endogenize" the probability of a person's vote being pivotal – to treat it not as fixed, but as an outcome of many voters' and candidates' strategic decisions. After all, people's sense of how likely they are to cast the deciding vote might well depend on how many other people they expect to turn out. Hence, Ledyard (1984) reasoned, if would-be voters have a general-equilibrium orientation and come to the conclusion that no one, in a large electorate, will turn out, then each one will infer that his or her chance of casting the deciding vote is high. If the benefits that will accrue when their side wins outweigh the costs of participation, they will vote (see also Medina 2007, 2018). But now their expectation again shifts and they anticipate high turnout. After all, everyone is making the same assumptions

---

[9] In fact, Riker and Ordeshook interpreted D as representing several "satisfactions" from "fulfilling one's civic duty to vote; complying with the ethic of voting; affirming allegiance to the political system; affirming a partisan preference; of deciding and going to the polls; and of affirming one's efficacy in the political system" (1968: 28).

and arriving at identical inferences, so now turnout will be high and the chances of casting a tie-breaking vote are again minuscule. So each person decides to save him or herself the trouble of going to the polls.

Is there any stable stopping point for this cycle? Ledyard analyzed a model with two candidates who try to attract voters by adopting popular policy positions. If the two candidates take different positions, Ledyard identified multiple equilibria – multiple stopping points – in which turnout is positive: at least someone votes. But this same model predicts that the two candidates will not remain apart, programmatically. Instead they converge to an identical policy position. Since now there is no utility differential over outcomes – the candidates' platforms are identical – "no one votes" (p. 23).[10]

Palfrey and Rosenthal (1983, 1985), in turn, treated people's *beliefs* about *p* as the outcome of a game. As in Ledyard (1984), a would-be voter predicts how many people will vote and therefore how likely he or she is to break a tie. Palfrey and Rosenthal's voters consider this problem from the standpoint of other voters. Palfrey and Rosenthal departed from Ledyard's model by assuming that candidates' positions are exogenous or fixed, and divergent from one another. Their key result is that, in large electorates, even if voters are uncertain about how costly it is for other people to vote and about others' preferences among candidates, there is no equilibrium with high turnout. They summarized their findings this way: "the outcome will essentially be determined by voters who, for unspecified reasons, find it *at least as costly to abstain as to vote*, regardless of the likelihood that their vote will affect the outcome of the election" (1985: 73, emphasis added). They lamented that "we have come full circle and are once again beset by the paradox of not voting" (p. 64).

How would rational choice theorists explain the behavior of George, our hypothetical voter? We imagined him earlier as an on-and-off, marginal voter. Riker and Ordeshook might have explained his behavior in terms of a weak adherence to a norm that says, *You should vote*. But the duty term is static in Riker and Ordeshook's model, like a personal trait that individuals carry around. So to explain variation – sometimes voting, sometimes abstaining – they would turn to the costs of voting and assume those that George faces vary across elections. It sometimes rains on Election Day, or George has a busy day that makes it hard to get to the polls, or his car is in the shop and he can't get a ride. On days like these, George's sense of voting as a duty is not strong enough to counterbalance the costs and inconveniences of going to the polls. When the weather is good and transportation easy, his sense of a duty is strong enough to get him to the polls.

A factor that will *not* make a difference in George's turnout behavior is how much he sees as at stake in the election: how much he likes one candidate over the leading competitor, whether he feels strongly about social programs

---

[10] In the equilibria he discerned with positive turnout, the sufficient conditions for their uniqueness were unknown.

or other public policies, and how they will be shaped by the outcome of an election.[11] As long as George is rational and holds no illusion that his vote will change the outcome, these factors will not come into his calculus of participation.

Minimax regret. Other theorists diverge more sharply from the assumptions of Downs, and Riker and Ordeshook, and succeed in generating good predictions, including widespread turnout in large electorates and a propensity to vote that varies with the importance of the election. Ferejohn and Fiorina (1974) propose that, instead of utility maximizers, would-be voters are "regret minimizers." People who follow a *minimax regret* decision-rule focus on avoiding the outcome that, should it come to pass, will cause them the greatest unhappiness (or regret about the decision they made). In the case of elections, according to Ferejohn and Fiorina, the greatest regret is to have abstained in one that ends in a tie. To forestall such an eventuality, the minimax decision-maker votes.

If his calculus is driven by minimax considerations, our marginal voter, George, will go about deciding whether to vote in quite a different way than he would have, had he followed the logic of rational choice theorists like Riker and Ordeshook. He would pose for himself the question, *What if I abstain and the election ends in a tie – how much will I regret not having voted?* The answer will be driven by how much he sees as at stake, the equivalent of *B* in the Riker–Ordeshook model, and he will weigh these stakes against the costs of voting. If, say, he is sure that the future of a social program he cares deeply about is on the line but he's busy at work, he may leave early or rush to the polls when his workday ends. If he sees no real difference between the candidates and their positions, he won't bother. He is not more likely to turn out if public opinion polls and the media report that it looks very close. He always assumes a hypothetical tie and works backward from that outcome.

Our own model, presented later in this chapter, shares with minimax regret the idea that there are psychic costs of abstention and that these costs grow in tandem with the utility a person enjoys from her preferred candidate's winning. But Ferejohn and Fiorina's assumptions about perceptions of the likelihood of a tie are untenable, a point made by contemporaneous critics. Mired in a dense fog of uncertainty, the minimax decision-maker in effect places highly unlikely events (a tied election) on an equal footing with very common ones

---

[11] Drawing on spatial models of voting, there is a sizable literature suggesting that the nature of the alternatives offered to voters might factor into their turnout decision, e.g., Brody and Page (1973), Zipp (1985), Adams and Merrill (2003), Plane and Gershtenson (2004), and Adams et al. (2006). In particular, voters are expected to be less likely to turn out when they perceive candidates' or parties' policy positions to be too similar to each other (*indifference*) or too distant from the voter's ideal position (*alienation*). Yet such accounts have a hard time explaining why the rational individual in their spatial model should bother to turn out, even if he or she feels strongly about one candidate over another (high *B* in our model), given the minuscule probability of one's vote determining the election outcome.

(one candidate's winning by a sizable margin). That actors have "no knowledge of the probabilities of various outcomes" is no more true, in Beck's view, than the "assumption of perfect information about these probabilities made in the decision making under risk model" (1975: 918). "If a minimax-regretter is going to dip down six factors of ten in probability to pick up the possibility that his sole vote may decide a presidential election," Stephens commented archly, "it is difficult for me to see that he will not dip down another factor of ten and pick up the possibility that he will be run over" by a car on his way to or from the polls.[12]

So here we have a model that makes good predictions: people turn out to vote, and their incentives to do so grow as the value they place on their preferred outcome grows. But the theory is built on assumptions that are untenable, even absurd; so one keeps looking for a better theory.

Expressive voting. Sometimes consumers buy a particular product or brand to tell others something about themselves, more than because they enjoy consuming it. A fancy car model might be more comfortable and handle better but a Subaru says, "I'm a sober individual of progressive tastes." This insight has been applied to political behavior. In Schuessler's (2000a, 2000b) formulation, "individuals do not necessarily participate in collective action in order to produce outcomes, but instead often do so in order to express who they are by attaching themselves to such outcomes" (2000b: 5).[13] The utility people enjoy from expressive voting is private and depends on their actually turning out to vote. Also, in Schuessler's formulation, it also depends on the number of others engaged in the same action. Hence expressive benefits play a role similar to duty in Riker and Ordeshook's model. Schuessler reworked the classic voter utility function thus:

$$U = (p)B - C + f_x(n_x), \qquad (2.3)$$

where U is the utility of voting and p, B, and C are the probability of a tie, the relative benefits of one's preferred candidate winning, and the costs of turning out, as in Riker and Ordeshook. Schuessler added n_x, the number of others voting for one's preferred candidate. The expression $f_x(n_x)$ replaced D, duty, in Riker and Ordeshook's revised model. To interpret the model in terms of its implications for George, he is more likely to turn out if he cares about signaling to others that he is the kind of person who votes (for his preferred candidate or party) and if he expects many others to do the same.

Expressive voting helps explain two real-life phenomena: positive turnout in large electorates, and *bandwagons* (in which an individual becomes more likely to support a candidate the larger the number of others who also do).

---

[12] Stephens (1975: 914); see Ferejohn and Fiorina (1975) for their response.

[13] Brennan and Lomasky (1993) also analyzed expressive voting, which in their treatment was more solipsistic than Schuessler's. Their voters were equally interested in acting in a manner consistent with their own self-image, and were free to do so because so little is at stake in their own vote.

But it does not solve other problems. Notice that in Schuessler's formulation, the utility differential over outcomes – B, how much a person cares about who wins and who loses – is still irrelevant to turnout decisions, because the product $(p)B$ is only imperceptibly greater than zero. Schuessler's formulation implies that we care only about whom we vote for and who wins to the degree that we are thus telling others about ourselves. Economic and social policy, religious attitudes of candidates, their characters, and personal qualities – none of these things in itself moves us to go to the polls.

Groups, parties, and networks. Collective action obstacles to participation fall away if the electorate is divided into groups, each of which contains enough members to influence the outcome of the election, and whose leaders use sticks and carrots to get their members to the polls. Uhlaner (1989), Morton (1987, 1991), and Shachar and Nalebuff (1999) offer models of this kind. It is not a leap to suppose that leaders will work harder to get their followers to the polls when the leader feels that more is at stake in the outcome. Utility differentials over outcomes thus come back into play but at the level of leaders, not the general electorate.

But *how* leaders mobilize followers is a question that group theories of participation do not satisfactorily answer. Vote buying was a solution in the era of machine politics. But in advanced democracies, the era of vote buying ended long ago (see Stokes et al. 2013). What's more, once we move from the world of a handful of powerful leaders distributing rewards, to the decentralized world of social pressure, collective action problems reappear. "Social pressure presumably relies on followers to reward and punish each other at the direction of the leader," wrote Feddersen (2004: 107). But "if exerting social pressure is costly to followers, it is not clear how this solves the problem, since followers will have the same incentive to shirk on exerting social pressure that they do to shirk on voting in the first place."

Another obvious agent of mobilization is the political party or campaign. No actor has a clearer interest in stimulating participation, especially of friendly voters. But, as we shall see in Chapter 3, there is evidence that party mobilization is less powerful than the internalized reasons people have for voting. Party-mobilization accounts must answer a series of questions, well enumerated by Rolfe (2012: 100): "Why are individuals who are mobilized, directly or indirectly, more likely to vote? Why do individuals respond to campaigns? How do campaigns affect individual decision making?"

Rolfe's answers zeroed in on social networks as agents of mobilization. Network theories of voter mobilization have attracted much recent interest (Abrams, Iversen, and Soskice 2010, Sinclair 2012). Whereas *groups* as agents of voter mobilization had identifiable leaders who somehow directed, coerced, or prodded their members to vote, social networks are informal and do the work of mobilization in more subtle and spontaneous ways. In Rolfe's *social theory of voting*, people take their cues from their family, friends, and acquaintances. They turn out to vote because they are embedded in social networks that push them to take part. Furthermore, the more important the election, the harder parties work to expand these networks. This activity is crucial because "larger social networks increase the likelihood that low-cost cooperative behaviors, such as turnout, will snowball, and thus ultimately increase aggregate turnout rates" (2012: 100). Likewise, in Abrams, Iversen, and Soskice's *informal social network* theory of turnout, "if politics is seen as important during an election period in one's network of friends and family, then voting gains social approval and not voting leads to social disapproval" (2010: 234).[14]

What doesn't ring true in network theories is that the would-be voter in the network will be no more responsive to messages coursing through it, whether they think profoundly bad things will happen should the wrong candidate win or when they are especially inspired by their favored one.[15] Abrams et al. explicitly modeled turnout levels as unrelated to B, which they defined as Riker and Ordeshook did. The same is true of a model developed by Gerber, Green, and Larimer (2008). The latter authors had a startling field experiment in which they boosted participation by around 8 percentage points by threatening to shame would-be abstainers. Gerber and his coauthors explained this result in terms of a shaming model. Voters derive rewards from voting that are both intrinsic (the subjective satisfaction of complying with one's civic duty) and socially imposed (the shame of being caught not complying with a norm). The more a person values complying with the norm of civic duty, other things being equal, the more likely she is to turn out. Furthermore, the more sensitive she is to social shaming, the more likely she is to vote. But these effects are independent of the importance she ascribes to the outcome; as in traditional calculus-of-voting models, B only influences participation choices in the highly unlikely event of a tie.[16]

---

[14] In Abrams and coauthors' formalization, B has no direct effect on voters' turnout decisions, only ones that run through social networks or campaigns. Abrams et al. (2010: 240) wrote, "the $P_i B_i$ term should have no practical influence since the probability of i's vote being pivotal is effectively zero ... " though – anticipating Rolfe – parties may focus more resources on mobilizing turnout when they see much as at stake and the outcome as close. But the importance of the outcome has no direct mobilizing effect on individual would-be voters.

[15] The work of Diana Mutz (especially Mutz 2002) is distinctive – and closer to the effect of social networks and pressure in our model – in that it implies that networks transmit real content about policies and candidates.

[16] If D_I is the intrinsic reward and D_E the extrinsic one, the authors offered the following linear approximation of voters' utilities from voting:

$$U(D_I, D_E) \approx \beta_1 D_I + \beta_2 D_E. \qquad (2.4)$$

If π_r is the probability that a potential voter perceives of others' learning whether he has voted, and if α is a constant weight that a voter attaches to the extrinsic consequences of voting, the calculus-of-voting equation can be rewritten as

$$pB + \beta_1 D_I + \alpha \pi_r + \beta_3 \pi_r D_I > C. \qquad (2.5)$$

Rolfe's theory is distinctive, as we have seen, in that political parties manipulate networks, making them grow by investing effort and resources in them. Yet here, too, all of the action takes place without anyone being aroused to care about what it means to have one or another candidate prevail. Consider again how the model might influence our marginal voter, George, to get to the polls. His daughter's friend might work for a campaign and suggest to his daughter that she try to get her whole family to the polls. But this mobilization happens without any discussion of the candidates, their qualities, or their positions. Thus social network theories in effect reduce the content of candidates' messages, ads, and appeals to focal points; ones that merely influence people's expectations about what their fellow citizens will do, not what politicians will do if they win.

Rule-utilitarian models. We turn now to a rule-utilitarian theory of voting. They produce realistic comparative statics: positive turnout in large electorates, turnout rates that rise with the importance of the election, and rates that rise with the expected closeness of the result. The theory's drawbacks lie in assumptions on which it is built, not in its predictions.

According to rule utilitarians, people decide whether or not to vote not by thinking about their personal costs and benefits in an ego-oriented way, nor about the impact their own vote will have on the outcome. Instead they adopt the vantage point of a welfare-maximizing social planner (Feddersen and Sandroni 2006) or of the leaders of their party or identity group (Coate and Conlin 2004).[17] In Feddersen and Sandroni's model, a subset of the electorate is comprised of *ethical* types, who adopt the vantage point of the social planner. The remainder of citizens, called *abstainers*, consider their own costs and benefits and feel no duty to take part. The abstainers are like citizens in the stripped-down rational choice models and do not vote. Ethical types (and abstainers) fall into two groups: those who believe that candidate 1's policies are the best for society, and those who believe that candidate 2's policies are best. There is uncertainty about the relative numbers of supporters of 1 and 2.

When ethical voters "do their part" (2006: 1274), they receive a payoff (d), a factor reminiscent of the duty term in standard models. Three factors influence levels of turnout: the importance of the election (w, like B in the standard model); the probability that candidate 1 wins (p – not, in this model, an individual's chances of breaking a tie); and the expected cumulative cost of voting, ψ, assessed across all of the members of one's group (e.g., across all ethicals who view candidate 2 as superior). Turnout is higher when the

---

[17] In so doing, they are following Harsanyi (1977, 1980). Feddersen and Sandroni called theirs a *rule-utilitarian* theory: their ethical citizens follow a rule that, if followed by all citizens, would maximize aggregate utility. Coate and Conlin called theirs a *group-rule-utilitarian* theory, one in which the rule, if followed, would maximize the utility of all members of the group. See Coate and Conlin (2004), pp. 1477–8, fn. 2.

election is important, the race is close, and the cumulative costs of voting are low.

So the model produces just the right comparative statics. But it rests on a key and unlikely assumption. This is the way in which costs come into the picture. People bear costs as individuals, but these individual costs only influence their turnout decisions indirectly. Ethical types do *not* seek to minimize their own costs; they seek to minimize the cumulative costs for the electorate as a whole. "We assume," wrote Feddersen and Sandroni, "that all agents prefer the social cost of voting to be minimized. So, if the agent were a social planner, then, holding constant the probability that candidate 1 wins the election, he prefers low turnout to minimize the social costs of voting" (2006: 1273). Coate and Conlin wrote, "not everybody should vote because that would result in *a surfeit of votes, imposing unnecessary costs on society*" (2004: 1479, emphasis added).

What's missing is a countervailing cumulative cost of abstention – a sense that things are amiss if very few people go to the polls. If one set of partisans outnumbers the other greatly and there is low probability of the minority-supported candidate prevailing, then the normatively preferable outcome is very low levels of turnout – approaching zero, asymptotically.[18] The social planner's goal, after all, is to mobilize just enough votes for the right side to win. By this route, rule utilitarians arrive at a conditional *duty to abstain*.[19] This duty kicks in for an ethical actor when his turning out to vote would increase the social cost of the election without producing a sufficiently large, offsetting increase in the probability of the best candidate winning.[20]

How would a voter like our hypothetical George decide whether to vote, in the world of rule utilitarianism? If he were to vote at all, he would be an ethical type, not an abstainer – they never vote. On the assumption that the relevant groups are partisans and George is, say, a Democrat, and one who is pondering whether to vote in a presidential election, if he lives in a state that

[18] If voters perceive little difference, in social welfare terms, between one or the other candidate's prevailing, very low turnout, approaching zero, is also the preferred outcome in these models.

[19] Group utilitarians end up with the unlikely construct of a duty to abstain because they need to incorporate costs into their model. Were there no costs to voting, or were the duty to vote simply to override these costs, all ethical voters would always vote, and the model would explain (unvarying) turnout among a segment of the population by assumption about their type. The awkwardness arises because rule utilitarianism begins with an agent who is socially oriented, not ego-oriented. Having built their theory around an ethical agent, the theorists seem wary of conjuring a more individually focused citizen when it comes to weighing up the costs of voting.

[20] The authors noted that their theoretical results will not be affected by having some agents prefer high turnout. "We only require that *some* agents prefer to minimize social costs" (p. 1273, fn 3, emphasis in the original). Though they do not present such a modification of their model, it is intuitive that the smaller the number of ethical actors who seek to avoid "extra" turnout – following instead the rule *always vote* – the weaker the relevant comparative statics.

is "safe" for Democrats and his personal costs of voting are high, his duty *not* to vote may kick in and he stays home. If he lives in a battleground state, or in a majority Republican state, it would be more likely that his duty would be to vote and he would comply with that duty (we shall have occasion to test some of these comparative statics in Chapter 3).

The duty to minimize cumulative costs of turnout runs counter to democratic theory. Where rule utilitarians want to minimize turnout so as to reduce social costs, democratic theorists want to minimize costs so as to maximize turnout. Indeed, democratic theorists see positive value in the act of voting, and consider high rates of enfranchisement and participation as definitional of democracy. They offer several reasons why we should favor near-full turnout. One has to do with the "principle of equal consideration of interests," which holds that "during a process of collective decision-making, the interests of every person who is subject to the decision must ... be accurately interpreted and made known."[21] Democratic theorists also see participation as educating and edifying the participants. For society too, there are collective benefits to near-full participation. So much so, in the view of Karlan (1994), that people should be paid to vote, as in the United States they are paid to perform jury duty. Compulsory voting systems implicitly institutionalize the idea that there is social value in getting every eligible citizen to vote.

Rule utilitarians' error is not in supposing that voting is costly, that people's decisions are sensitive to these costs, or that some people will be justified in abstaining because their individual costs of participation are high. The error, in our view, is to omit an imperative to minimize abstention (or maximize participation). What is needed are two imperatives: one that says *maximize turnout*, and another that says, *avoid imposing unnecessary costs*. The model that we develop later features individual-level equivalents to both rules: people bear costs both when they participate and when they abstain.

Finally, group utilitarians envision actors who are driven mainly by moral imperatives; or, more accurately, it envisions a population polarized between those untouched by moral imperatives and those whose actions are driven entirely by them. Our George has become a rather philosophical fellow. Of course this is an abstract, mathematical model; yet it should be possible to explain political participation with recourse to actors who are more recognizably three-dimensional and psychologically nuanced than the types we have been encountering.

To summarize, after the shift from mainly social-psychological to economic orientations toward turnout, decision- and game-theoretic models failed to predict observed patterns of voting. They make little sense of the stimulating effect of utility differentials over outcomes on people's willingness to vote. The

---

[21] Dahl (1989: 86). For a recent statement, see Kolodny (2014: 289). Uncertainty about the distribution of supporters of each candidate is an explicit feature of the rule-utilitarian model, so without an election, the preferences of individuals cannot be "made known."

minimax regret decision model does make sense of it; but this model rests on unrealistic assumptions about the degree of voters' uncertainty when they consider election outcomes. Party and civil-society leaders may work harder to mobilize their bases when much is at stake, and the outcome seems close, but why their efforts are fruitful, and how the system of mobilization sidesteps free-riding at all levels, have not been adequately explained. Network models paint a picture of citizens who care only about social approbation or shame while remaining unmoved by policy proposals or the quality of candidates. This limitation reduces the power of expressive models, as well. Rule utilitarianism is promising in that it produces all of the right comparative statics. But it founders, in our view, on counterintuitive decision-rules, ones that real-life voters are unlikely to follow.

THE COSTLY ABSTENTION THEORY OF TURNOUT

Having identified a series of strengths and shortcomings in prior theories, we now offer a new one. Our approach is decision- rather than game-theoretic. Recall that early rational choice treatments (Downs; Riker and Ordeshook; Ferejohn and Fiorina) used decision theory, whereas a later, game-theoretic line of research treated voters as making decisions in anticipation of other voters' choices. In this later work, voters' strategic orientation arose from their presumed concern with whether their vote would break a tie.[22] Our voters do not think about breaking a tie. They are sensitive to the strategic context of the election in that they experience greater urgency and engagement when the outcome seems likely to be close. But this kind of strategic sensitivity does not imply an interdependence of voters' actions as modeled, for instance, by Ledyard (1984).[23] For these reasons we focus on the independent decision calculi of voters, where the contextual factors of the election, like its competitiveness, are exogenously determined.

The factors influencing people's turnout decisions include:

- their costs of abstention (A), which are intrinsic or psychological costs;
- their costs of participation (C);
- extrinsic social pressures and civic expectations of participation (D_E);
- the value they place on their preferred candidate or party winning (B); and

[22] Recall, however, that the game-theoretic approach did not indicate equilibria with high turnout in large electorates, unless voters derived private rewards from voting.

[23] Our decision-theoretic treatment of turnout does not preclude the collective action nature of elections (Aldrich 1993). Parties and campaigns certainly strategize, but individual voters take the parties' actions as givens; hence we set aside party actions in the theory elaborated next. Population-wide outcomes can be derived from our model by aggregating individual choices. But these outcomes derive in straightforward ways from the population distributions of each parameter in the model. Therefore, little is added to the analysis by moving from individual to cumulative predictions.

- the strategic context of the election – their perceptions of the likely closeness of the result, i.e., its competitiveness (γ).

The relationships among these factors and their effect on the rewards from participating, P, can be expressed in the following system of equations:

$$P = A - C + D_E, \tag{2.6}$$

$$A = f(B[1 + \gamma]), \quad f'(\cdot) > 0. \tag{2.7}$$

Equation [2.6] lays out the net rewards of participating over abstaining. By participating, one incurs the costs of participation but also reaps benefits that follow from conforming to civic expectations of participation (or from avoiding social sanctions for abstaining). Hence the utility from participation is $(-C + D_E)$. Note that individuals in our framework are not motivated by the possibility (or illusion) of their vote changing the outcome of the election; therefore a term akin to $p(B)$ in the Riker–Ordeshook framework is not relevant. Turning to abstention, we posit that it can impose costs as well, as we explain shortly. Therefore, the utility from abstaining is not zero but given by $(-A)$. The difference between $(-C + D_E)$ and $(-A)$ gives us the net rewards of participation over abstention, $(A - C + D_E)$.

In what follows, we explain the factors in equations [2.6] and [2.7], and the relationships among them.

The costs of abstention (A). Our concept of costs of abstention rests on a simple but key idea: just as voting imposes costs on individuals, abstaining imposes costs as well, quite apart from any effect a person sees her vote as having on the outcome. That is, she can experience straight-up disutility from not taking part, and the desire to avoid such disutility can induce her to participate.

The costs of abstention are subjective and psychological.[24] They are incurred when people suffer a psychic tension, or dissonance, upon failing to take part in collective action or anticipate failing to do so, even if they know their action would have a minuscule impact on the eventual outcome. To give a sense of the intuition here, one of the authors notes that she is worried about climate change – that humans may have already done irreversible damage and that the adverse effects of global warming are already visible and will eventually be devastating. This worry makes her conscious of ways in which her family wastes fossil fuels and contributes greenhouse gases. If her spouse leaves their car idling unnecessarily and she is in the passenger seat, she experiences

---

[24] In certain circumstances one might think of benefits of abstention as well. For example, in elections that are considered to be not free and fair, there might be calls for a boycott. In turn, some individuals might be subject to a "moral" cost (intrinsic or extrinsic) if they participate, and the desire to avoid such disutility might be the benefit of abstention. We consider such circumstances as peripheral to our aim in this book, however. In our framework the benefits of abstention are just saving the costs of participation, and hence do not call for a separate treatment.

a subjective sensation that is very close to physical pain. She is liable to reach over and turn the key to the "off" position. Turning the car off, like many other small emissions-reducing actions that she or any other individual might take, is unlikely to make a discernible difference in global climate change. But even if she paused to ponder this fact, she might not be able to stop herself from turning the car off. Her reaction is not the result of moral reflection, though if she were to consider the moral dimensions of her actions her instinct to turn it off would be redoubled.

The act of turning off the car has equivalents in the world of electoral participation. When one cares about the outcome of an election, when one is engaged and has the feeling that much is at stake in the outcome, it is intuitive that one will need to take the same actions as many other people if the desired outcome is to be achieved. The costs of abstention are conceived as an increasing function of the differential utilities over outcomes, B, and the competitiveness of the election, γ, in our model.

How much do I care? Differential utilities over outcomes (B). In our theory, the value that would-be voters place on their preferred candidate or party winning (B) is a main driver of costs of abstention and hence of participation in elections. These differential benefits can run the gamut from tax advantages or improved public services, to the pleasure of one's party or ideological fellow traveler winning, to the relief experienced when a feared candidate loses. We "bring B back in" by recognizing its impact on the costs of abstention (A). It is not simply that the more people suffer if they abstain, the more likely they are to vote. If so, this would be yet another private benefit of voting, like D in the Riker–Ordeshook model, and would not help explain why differential utilities over outcomes influence people's decisions to participate. Our key point comes in equation [2.7]. It formalizes the idea that the costs of abstention are a positive function of B, the differential benefit a voter derives from the success of his or her most preferred candidate over others. That is, the magnitude of these costs rises and falls as a function of how much a person believes is at stake in the outcome. If he cares greatly about who wins and who loses, the cost of abstention will be high and his likelihood of voting increases. If he cares little, abstention is less costly and he is more likely to stay home. To put it more strongly, when one cares a lot about the outcome, it may be more burdensome or difficult to *keep oneself from participating* than it is to pay the kinds of costs usually attributed to voting.

By implying that the outcome of an election does not matter for individuals' turnout decisions, received theories of democracy rest on psychologically untenable grounds. They ask us to believe that a person can follow a campaign closely, see the fate of her family or her country as resting on its outcome, but, when Election Day comes, stay home and await the actions of others. Not only does this notion chafe against intuition, it fails to make sense of several hard facts about elections and voters, as demonstrated in Chapter 3. These facts make us skeptical of the idea that utility differentials over outcomes do not play a role in turnout.

The strategic context: Closeness (γ). The strategic context in which many people decide whether to vote or abstain has little to do with their likelihood of breaking a tie. Instead they are moved by the likely closeness of the finish. We define γ (the Greek letter gamma) as a would-be voter's perception of the likely closeness, or competitiveness, of the election.[25] In Chapter 3 we offer observational and experimental evidence that close races can be mobilizing – though only for people who care about the outcome. That is, for those who are disengaged or see the alternative outcomes of an election as not very different or important to them, it makes little difference whether the race is tight or one side seems clearly headed for victory. Blais (2000) reviewed 32 studies that considered the relationship between closeness of elections and turnout in different settings, and reported that closeness is associated with higher turnout in 27 of them. Intuition, backed by research (including our own, reported in Chapter 3), indicates that the close-result effect mainly comes into play for individuals who care about the outcome.

Several explanations have been proposed for the close-election effect on turnout. Ours, as reflected in equation [2.7], is that the prospect of sitting out an election about which one cares (high B) and that appears headed for a close finish drives up the costs of abstention.[26] For some this may be an automatic response to arousal, like cheering more intensely in a sports match that is close (an analogy drawn by Brennan and Lomasky 1993, 2000). Emotions like enthusiasm, fear, or anger are also amplified when the election is expected to be close, driving up costs of abstention. But for many, this greater intensity of feeling and urgency to act reflects their adoption of the vantage point of their preferred party or candidate. Thus voting often involves a kind of transference. This is especially the case for strong partisans or those with strong candidate preferences.

---

[25] While the closeness of an election has a more straightforward interpretation in two-candidate or two-party races than in multiparty elections, our model applies to multiparty elections as well. A would-be voter's perception of the closeness of a multiparty election might be shaped by several factors, depending on the electoral standing of his or her preferred party. For a supporter of the (likely) leading party in the election without a clear contender, the relevant factor may be the closeness of the party to obtain the majority of seats in the parliament to form a single-party government. In the case of two competitive major parties, the difference between their expected vote shares would be important, as the mandate to form the government might be given to the party with the largest vote share. Most multiparty systems have electoral thresholds for parties to obtain seats in parliament. Therefore supporters of smaller parties might perceive the closeness of the election in terms of the likelihood of their party of crossing this threshold, or sending a representative from their district to the parliament.

[26] Technically equation [2.7] could be more appropriately written as $A = f(B[k + \gamma])$, where $k > 0$ is a constant that indexes the importance of B relative to γ for a citizen's costs of abstention.

This, then, is party identification taken beyond affinity or policy preference to actually *seeing like a party*. People who see the strategic context as the party does are not focused on the impact of their own vote on the result when they are swayed by the prospects of a close race. Instead they are focused on electorate-wide patterns. This focus leads individuals to take part because it is natural to act in ways that are consistent with the course of events that one hopes transpires.

A different interpretation of the close-election effect, in the spirit of the Riker–Ordeshook model, is that during close races people overestimate the probability of a tie and are mobilized because they see a real chance of breaking it. Of course, in large electorates the probability that even a tight race will end in a tie is vanishingly small, so this interpretation casts voters as not entirely numerate. Riker and Ordeshook (1968: 38–9) noted that p is a subjective quantity, perhaps prone to being overestimated. In Chapter 3 we report on research, of others and our own, indicating that though a minority of voters in fact does overestimate p, the majority considers the possibility of a tie to be remote. Their subjective perceptions of the probability of a tie do not have much effect on the decision to turn out.

Yet another rival explanation to our own, which goes along the lines of group mobilization theories, is that the closeness effect works entirely through political elites. When an important race is tight, more campaign funds are raised, more ads are placed, and more direct mobilization efforts are undertaken. Though all of this is clearly true, still we shall offer evidence in Chapter 3 that voters themselves respond to close elections (as long as they are also important ones) and that they endure greater psychic costs of abstention in close races, even in the absence of elite mobilization.[27]

Costs of participation (C). Voters also bear costs when they participate. They expend resources and time to get to the polls and cognitive effort to figure out their views of the candidates and whom to support. In contrast to the rule-utilitarian models reviewed later, we assume that these costs sometimes dissuade people from voting, not because they have internalized a moral principle or norm that says, *Keep the social costs of voting low*, but simply because they wish to minimize these burdens on themselves.

Nearly all scholars agree that voting is costly and that these costs can be a real impediment to participation. In their excoriating review of rational choice theories of turnout, Green and Shapiro concede that if this theory offers

---

[27] To mention a few other rival explanations, political psychologists have uncovered some evidence of *diagnostic voting*: people who turn out believe that participation rates will be higher on their side and therefore are optimistic about their candidate winning (Quattrone and Tversky 1984, 1988, Acevedo and Krueger 2004). Some individuals do evince greater optimism about the result when they vote, and pessimism if they are kept from voting. There is less evidence of out-and-out *magical voting*, the belief that a person's vote will causally induce others to vote the same way (Acevedo and Krueger 2004).

any advantages over competing theories, they lie in its "ability to make clear predictions about the effects of increasing or decreasing the costs of voting" (1994: 70).

As noted in the first chapter, by taking into account the costs people bear when they participate as well as those they bear when they abstain, we can make sense of otherwise puzzling instances in which participation becomes more difficult or dangerous and yet participation *rises*. Consider voter ID laws. After a 2013 US Supreme Court decision loosened federal oversight of electoral laws, several southern states enacted laws requiring more stringent proof of eligibility to vote. These laws were suspected of being a strategy to suppress the vote among poor and African-American voters. They clearly raise the costs of voting. Many would-be voters need to bring birth certificates or other identification to the polls. Yet these laws appear to have other, countervailing effects. They anger the target population and thus encourage them to turn out (Valentino and Neuner 2016).[28] We submit that the laws drive up both the costs of participation *and* the costs of abstention, so that the net impact on turnout was small. The same dynamic appears in social movements, as we shall see in Chapter 5. Police crackdowns can scare bystanders off but also anger them and hence encourage them to join. Cost-benefit analysis is incapable of making sense of this dynamic.

Extrinsic social norms and pressure (D_E). People might also pay externally imposed, social costs when they fail to turn out. Some of these are imposed by people in one's social network and involve personal ties. These are "the cost of saying 'no' when asked whether or not you voted" (Niemi 1976: 117). Social pressure can be subtle or it can be explicit; it comes from family, friends, coworkers, neighbors, or any relevant social group. Reporting the results of a large-scale get-out-the-vote field experiment, Gerber et al. (2008: 34) highlight that "exposing a person's voting record to his or her neighbors turns out to be an order of magnitude more effective than conventional pieces of partisan or nonpartisan direct mail." Yet pressure can be effective outside of networks, as well. We know that people portray themselves in socially desirable ways even before complete strangers, as the frequent overreporting of voting in surveys suggests (Holbrook and Krosnick 2010).

In short, any satisfactory theory of electoral participation should account for the force of social pressure.

---

[28] Citrin et al. (2014) conducted a field experiment in the areas of Tennessee and Virginia in which they sent out information to treatment groups alerting them to voter ID laws and found no evidence of a turnout effect. Highton's (2017) review suggested modest effects of strict voter identification laws on turnout. But Hajnal et al. (2017) found strong effects, with these laws depressing turnout among blacks and Hispanics by nine percentage points. Hajnal and coauthors' methods and findings were challenged by Grimmer et al. (2018; see the response by Hajnal et al. 2018). It should be noted that the change in laws is recent; only with time will we be able to assess the longer-term impact of these laws.

The duty to vote can also be considered under the rubric of social pressure. We follow Gerber et al. (2008) in decomposing this duty into intrinsic, D_I, and extrinsic, D_E, components:[29]

$$D = U(D_I, D_E), \tag{2.8}$$

where D_I captures the intrinsic satisfaction from complying with the norm that citizens in democracies should turn out to vote. To the extent that a person has internalized this norm, it falls under the rubric of costs of abstention. The internalized norm will encourage the person to vote, even if she does not anticipate being held to account by others for inaction. In turn, D_E refers to extrinsic incentives – social norms and pressures – that encourage a person to vote.

Our model thus takes into account extrinsic, social considerations that are independent of differential utilities over outcomes and of the closeness of the election; in equation [2.6], D_E influences P but is independent of B and of γ. Of course, people who see an election as extremely important may choose to exert a lot of pressure on their friends to go to the polls. They might persuade a would-be abstainer that the election is important, thus pushing their interlocutor's B upward. If so, in our model this makes the person who is the object of social pressure more likely to vote because B influences A, and A influences P. But D_E in our model indexes the added likelihood of voting by the person who is the target of social pressure, even when his own level of B is unaffected. To clarify, think about the situation from George's perspective. He is disengaged during an election campaign and doesn't see much at stake in the outcome; but his friends see a lot at stake and look at him askance when they have the impression that he may stay home on Election Day. So George's likelihood of turning out goes up because his D_E value rises. His friends' B values are high, but his remains low.

THE ROLE OF EMOTIONS

Psychologists have demonstrated that people's emotional responses can make them more or less likely to get involved in collective action.[30] The direction of the effect depends on which emotion is elicited. Psychologists label some emotions *approach emotions* and others *withdrawal emotions*; the former encourage those experiencing them to join in collective action, the latter discourage it (Carver 2004). Research establishing the causal effects of emotions on political engagement and action typically excludes the kinds of costs and

---

[29] Gerber et al. (2008: 35) wrote that "D_I is the intrinsic benefits associated with voting, a term that captures the positive feeling the voter experiences from fulfilling a civic duty ... and D_E is the extrinsic benefit from voting, a term which captures the social consequences of voting."

[30] In addition to the studies cited here, see also Marcus et al. (2000), Mutz (2002), and Valentino et al. (2011). Social-psychological research into the emotional underpinnings of protests and other costly actions is also germane, though its relevance to voting has not been fully explored. See e.g., Iyer et al. (2007), Thomas et al. (2009), and van Zomeren (2013).

other factors we have been discussing here. Instead it usually discerns partial, other-things-being-equal effects, which could be rendered thus:

$$P = f(E_A) - g(E_W), \tag{2.9}$$

where E_A indicates approach emotions and E_W withdrawal emotions.

An important and ongoing research task is to work out, among core emotions, which are approach and which withdrawal ones. A complicating fact, also reflected in the research agenda, is that external stimuli frequently elicit multiple emotions, as explained by Jasper (2014) in relation to social movement participation. Psychologists are in agreement that anger is an approach emotion; it drives people to participate in actions and induces them to ignore risks (Lerner and Keltner 2001, Carver and Harmon-Jones 2009). Anger is shaped not just by stimuli but by the interpretations and moral frames attached to them. Enthusiasm is also an approach emotion, tending to draw people to act in concert with others to support the source of their enthusiasm, while guilt and sadness tend to be withdrawal emotions (Carver 2004).

Beyond these emotions, there is greater ambiguity. Shame can lead people to avoid contact and hunker down in private spaces, but it can also encourage them to participate, as when they anticipate public shaming should they abstain (e.g., as in Gerber et al. 2008). Fear and anxiety also have ambiguous effects. They can lead people to be less risk-accepting and more cautious – more willing to invest in seeking out information and less prone to fall back on heuristics, such as those offered by partisanship (MacKuen et al. 2010). But people who become fearful can also be aroused to act to forestall outcomes that frighten them. What's more, fear and anger are closely related; when people are made fearful, they are also often made angry (Berkowitz and Harmon-Jones 2004). Valentino et al. (2009) hypothesized and provided evidence that individuals' internal efficacy (the extent to which one considers himself or herself competent and influential) might be relevant to whether they experience anger or fear in response to policy threats – high internal efficacy facilitates anger (as opposed to fear) in such circumstances, which in turn mobilizes individuals.

In the terms of the model we offered earlier, the impacts of emotions are complex and relate to several parameters. For example, the perceived relative positions of candidates and hence utility differentials over outcomes (B) can have an impact on emotions. Hutchings et al. (2006) exposed subjects to information highlighting sharply diverging policy positions of candidates whom they preferred and others they opposed. They measured much higher levels of enthusiasm for the preferred candidate among the members of the relevant treatment group. Similarly, MacKuen et al. (2010) found that individuals feel more enthusiastic when they find out that authorities adopted policy in line with their preferences. An increase in B, in these cases, stirs an approach emotion, which presumably increases people's willingness to act collectively.

The skeptic might react that "enthusiasm" and utility income are so close that they are actually different words for the same phenomenon. But causal effects between B and emotions can also travel in the opposite direction. Conover and Feldman (1986) tracked people's sometimes diverging reactions to the same economic information, with bad economic news generating anger among some and fear among others. But they also noted that people can initially process such information cognitively, later forget the information, but still retain the affective stance that the information originally evoked in them. In the same way that people can hold enduring grudges based on long-forgotten slights, they can retain an unfavorable view of politicians whom they associate with an economic downturn, even when the facts about the downturn become hazy and when the underlying conditions improve. In the terms of our model, a spike in B can be sustained through emotional rather than cognitive channels of causation, leading to a lasting ratcheting up of A and hence of the probability of participation.

If we were to incorporate these insights into our core formal model, the result would be a cumbersome proliferation of interactions and causal simultaneity. Focusing just on approach emotions, they undoubtedly can amplify costs of abstention. To make this intuitive, consider the example of George, whom we can imagine as a calm, unemotional fellow. But George has a brother who is more easily agitated.[31] A candidate appears whom both brothers find distasteful and would like to see defeated. If the siblings had to estimate a quantity for B, it would be roughly the same. Cool-headed George will experience higher A – more dissonance at the prospect of staying away from the polls – than he would if B were smaller. But the distasteful candidate rouses George's brother to a high pitch of anger, which amplifies his costs of abstention; the increment in his willingness to vote is much greater than George's. Emotions are undoubtedly related to γ, as well. Continuing with the same hypothetical example, if the election looks like it will be close, cerebral George keeps abreast of public opinion polls and is unlikely to stay home, come Election Day. But his reactive brother is raised to heights of fear and anger at the palpable possibility that the obnoxious candidate may win; he will now certainly vote, come hell or high water.

Hence, if we were to insert a parameter for emotions into our formal model, it would appear as a potential magnifier of the impact of utility benefits as well as closeness on the costs of abstention, either intensifying these costs or dampening them, depending on the nature of the emotion.[32]

Since both the magnitude and the direction of emotional effects on turnout are subject to manipulation, we also expect ambitious politicians to try to mold people's emotions. We will see a concrete example later in this study. A stimulus, losing one's job, provokes withdrawal emotions when politicians

---

[31] For recent research on differences in emotional intensity across individuals, see Larsen et al. (2002), Acevedo et al. (2014), and Eres et al. (2015).

[32] That is, the literature reviewed here would lead one to expect that a campaign that increased sadness or anxiety, generally found to be withdrawal emotions, would reduce costs of abstention and tend to keep those experiencing them at home.

stay away from the subject but approach emotions when they pay attention to it, constructing a moral and causal framework of blame around it. The consequences for collective action, with and without this framework, are starkly different.

SUMMARY: THE THEORY OF COSTLY ABSTENTION

How does the theory of electoral participation presented in the preceding pages differ from earlier ones? Three features of our theory are especially distinctive and allow us to make better sense of observed facts about turnout.

One is that we emphasize not just the costs of participation, but also the *costs of abstention*. Though costs of this kind appear, implicitly, in the duty concept of rational choice theory or in the social pressures entailed in network theories, we have explicitly linked them to people's perceptions of the importance of the election.[33] As the costs of abstention are intrinsic and psychological, we can incorporate *emotional responses* of individuals to politics into our theory. The recognition that people turn out to vote because doing so can help them avoid frustration and psychic discomfort is an important departure from prior models.

Second, whereas social-psychological and rational choice models considered people's feeling of a civic duty to vote as an encouragement to collective action, we add the observation that responsiveness to this norm may reflect either social pressure or internalization of the norm (or a mix of the two). Individuals who have internalized the norm will be more likely to vote even when they do not think about being held to account, after the fact, by other actors or by people in their social networks. To the extent that it operates for extrinsic reasons, it is one of a series of social pressures that also encourage turnout. Our theory postulates that an internalized sense of duty grows and abates in tandem with how much the individual views as at stake in an election. In this sense it is a cost of abstention. That duty is a conditional, not an absolute norm, is a proposition that we test in Chapter 3.

Third, we hold that voters think not about ties but about *close races*. When an election that they deem important also looks close, the costs of abstention mount. Close, important races are more rousing, as are close, important sports matches; and when voters "see like a party" they naturally want to take part. Elites also mobilize more actively in close races, but we hold that many voters react to tight contests, even without elite intermediation.

Finally, events or situations that boost the costs of participation that people face sometimes also boost their costs of abstention. That actual turnout will be driven by net costs helps explain dynamics that are not easily explained within the bounds of theories in which only participation imposes costs.

---

[33] Or, more generically, to the utility differentials over outcomes that the would-be voter perceives.

3

Testing the Costly Abstention Theory of Turnout

In this chapter we subject our theory of costly abstention and voter turnout to empirical testing. The theory stipulates that turnout rises when people perceive that a lot is at stake in the outcome of the contest, more so when important contests are also close-run. They participate not just because they are prodded by campaigns or face shaming from neighbors if they stay home. Instead they have intrinsic reasons for turning out when they care about the outcome. Internalized drives can get them to the polls, drives that are intensified by emotions like anger or enthusiasm. Norms of civic duty play a role, but they, too, are conditional on how much the would-be voter sees as at stake in the contest. These intrinsic reactions are costs of abstention; in this chapter we offer evidence that these costs are quite real.

We present evidence that we have gathered and also draw on a rich secondary literature about turnout in democracies around the world. The mix of observational, survey, and experimental evidence allows us to disentangle extrinsic mobilization effects from intrinsic psychological ones, delve into the emotional fallout of abstention, and probe norms as a dynamic factor in people's turnout decisions.

OBSERVATIONAL EVIDENCE ABOUT UTILITY DIFFERENTIALS AND CLOSENESS

The Importance of the Contest

Ask a non-social scientist why she votes in mass elections and she's likely to tell you her hopes about what will happen if her favored candidate wins and her fears about what will happen if he doesn't. If she thinks your own participation is in doubt, she may implore you to consider the composition of the courts, or public spending priorities, or legislation defining citizens' rights and obligations. If she's less focused on policy but still politically engaged, she may remind you about the personality strengths and flaws of the candidates.

Ask an empirically minded scholar of electoral participation what distinguishes people who regularly turn out from those who do not and you are likely to get a response that is not inconsistent with the layperson's account. People who are engaged in politics and who see the outcome of elections as important are much more likely to participate, even controlling for other predictive factors such as partisanship, education, or income (e.g., Rosenstone and Hansen 1993, Verba et al. 1995, Leighley and Nagler 2014).

But ask a theorist of turnout and you're likely to get a different answer. Theoretically oriented social scientists have had to work harder to make sense of the lay account. As we saw in Chapter 2, rational choice theorists discount the effect of individuals' differential utilities over outcomes, what we will call the *B* effect. So do mobilization models. In the latter, instead of *B* directly influencing citizens' decisions whether to vote or abstain, its impact is mediated by another actor – a political party or campaign, a group or organization leader, or a social network – that will work especially hard at mobilization when the stakes are high.

These are serious shortcomings. Beyond lay intuitions, there are good empirical grounds to believe that *B* plays a big part in bringing people to the polls, and that it plays this role even when people are not being actively mobilized by other actors. Consider the following facts.

More people, on average, turn out to vote in democracies around the world when the office being filled is national rather than regional or local. Also, more turn out when the national office being filled is for the head of government than for the national legislature (Blais 2000, 2006, Przeworski 2009). So if people perceive there is more at stake the more elevated the office being filled, these patterns are an indication that *B* matters. Blais (2000: 40) offers relevant evidence from a range of presidential democracies around the world. He finds turnout usually to be higher in presidential than legislative elections. The differences are often large: 14 percentage points, for instance, in France and Finland in the 1990s. Blais also shows that turnout in local elections around the world generally lags that in national elections. Again the gaps are often large: 38 percentage points, on average, in New Zealand, 34 percentage points in Britain, and 20 in Israel (2000: 37). In the United States, the sawtooth pattern in Figure 3.1 shows the dramatic difference in turnout between presidential and midterm congressional elections, between 1960 and 2016. The average difference across pairs of elections is about 18 percentage points.[1]

---

[1] Blais et al. (2000: 185–6) found that respondents in a 1995 British Columbia survey viewed the outcome of provincial elections as more important than those of their ridings. In turn, Franklin (2004: 96) has shown that turnout tends to be higher in elections in which "the political complexion of the executive is responsive to the choices made at the time of the election" – a negative case being Switzerland since the early 1960s, in which the same governing coalition wins year after year, whatever the outcome of legislative elections. Franklin and Hirczy (1998) also pointed out that if voters participate in part to influence the course of public policy, then they should turn out at lower rates under institutional conditions of a separation of powers

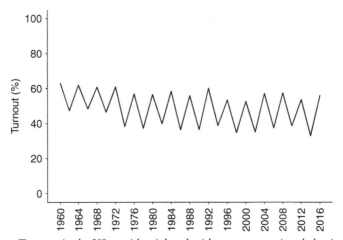

FIGURE 3.1 Turnout in the US presidential and midterm congressional elections, 1960–2016.
Source: International Institute for Democracy and Electoral Assistance (IDEA).

Perhaps it is simply the case that parties and campaigns work harder to mobilize voters in high-level elections, as proposed by mobilization theorists. But to the extent that the *level* of the office being filled is distinguishable from parties' *mobilization efforts* as factors boosting turnout, high-office elections trump mobilization, handily. In a meta-analysis of get-out-the-vote field experiments in the United States, Arceneaux and Nickerson (2009) concluded that high-salience (national) elections more than triple the probability of an average person's turning out to vote, compared to low-salience (local) ones. By contrast, intensive mobilization through face-to-face canvassing, the most effective technique, increases turnout on average by about 10 percentage points. Most interventions have much smaller effects.

There is more evidence that high-office effects on turnout are not all about campaign mobilization efforts but also – and more importantly – about people's perception that much is at stake in these elections. Some comes from a comparison of turnout for US national elections in "battleground" versus "safe" states.[2] Presidential campaigns invest heavily in get-out-the-vote efforts in battleground states. Their efforts in safe states are negligible by comparison. Between 1988 and 2008, 80% of presidential candidate visits and spending on advertising went to battleground states (Shaw 2006); in 2008, the two major presidential campaigns poured 98% of their total spending, more than one billion dollars, into battleground states (Gerber et al. 2009).

and even more so when systems of such separation have divided government. They found that turnout was indeed lower in the United States, between 1840 and 1992, in periods of divided government.

[2] Battleground states are ones where the state-level race is predicted to be close, and therefore the electoral college votes it possesses, in most states allotted by a winner-take-all rule, are up for grabs.

These investments do increase turnout, but the effects are modest. Gerber et al. (2009) report that turnout was on average two percentage points higher in battleground states than in safe states in presidential elections from 1980 to 2008. This battleground–safe state turnout differential pales in comparison to the difference in turnout between presidential and midterm congressional elections, which was on average 16 percentage points during the same period. Gerber and his coauthors concluded that "turnout is primarily linked to factors affecting the entire electorate, such as *the social importance of presidential elections*, rather than factors that influence just a portion of the country, such as intensive campaigning and mobilization efforts or a greater chance of casting a decisive vote" (2009: 13, emphasis added).

Individual-level observational studies of voter turnout strongly suggest that the importance of the election matters. In the United States, this was a key finding in *The American Voter*, and it has echoed through many studies since. Analyzing American National Election Studies (ANES) surveys conducted between the 1950s and 1980s, Rosenstone and Hansen (1993) found that people who reported caring a great deal about which party wins had a 6.4% greater probability of voting; people who reported strong affect for a party had a 11.4% greater probability of voting; and those who had a strong affect for a candidate had a 5.6% greater probability of turning out. In the 2004 presidential election, intensity of feelings about the incumbent, whether negative or positive, significantly increased a person's probability of voting (Abramowitz and Saunders 2008).[3] Interest in elections has been shown to have a similarly powerful impact on participation in British elections. Whiteley et al. (2013) found expressed interest to be a more powerful predictor of verified participation in the 2010 British national election than was educational level, occupation, or exposure to political campaigns.

Cross-national studies indicate that institutional features related to the importance of elections influence turnout. This point was highlighted by Jackman (1987: 407), who proposed that "institutional arrangements influence the degree to which potential voters think their vote will make a difference both to the election outcome itself and to the subsequent formation of a government." He hypothesized that unicameralism should increase turnout as it furnishes a clearer link between elections and legislation, and a larger number of political parties should depress turnout as it renders elections less decisive for government formation, given the greater likelihood of coalition governments. Jackman analyzed turnout levels across 19 established democracies in the 1960s and 1970s and found evidence of both unicameralism (positive) and multiparty (negative) effects.

Several subsequent studies reported similar findings. Blais (2000) studied a much larger sample, 324 lower-house elections held in 91 countries between

---

3 Mutz (2002) provided similar evidence from two representative national surveys in the United States – individuals who are more ambivalent about the candidates are less likely to vote.

1972 and 1995. He found that turnout is higher when the parliamentary election is more decisive – when there is no president or upper house and when the system is not a federation. Tavits (2009) studied turnout in 288 parliamentary elections held across the globe between 1946 and 2006. Turnout was lower in systems in which there was also a directly elected head-of-state (i.e., president). She attributed this difference in part to election fatigue but also to a downgrading of the importance of parliamentary elections in people's minds when they also can elect the president. In turn, Franklin (2004) argued – and provided evidence – that turnout in legislative elections moves in tandem with "executive responsiveness – the extent to which the political complexion of the executive is responsive to the choices made at the time of an election" (p. 96). Recently, Kasara and Suryanarayan (2015) found that wealthy citizens turn out at lower rates than the poor in many developing democracies, reversing the positive impact of income on turnout found in advanced democracies. Their explanation is that weak states in the developing world tax the wealthy at relatively low rates. Because little is at stake for the wealthy in these countries, they are comparatively disinclined to vote. All of these studies imply that institutional factors influence turnout by raising or diminishing the importance of the electoral contest in the eyes of voters.

Campaigns spend much time explaining why the outcome matters. Anyone who pays attention to campaigns might have the sense that candidates spend a good deal of time emphasizing the utility differential between the world under their leadership compared to the world governed by their opponents.

Our research supports this impression. We coded 1,266 statements in stump speeches by 18 US presidential candidates who ran for office between 1980 and 2012. Following the Riker–Ordeshook notation, we coded some campaign statements as *B*-statements – ones that emphasize the importance of the outcome. In *B*-statements, candidates implicitly say "vote for me because I will bring about better outcomes," or "vote for me because my opponent will bring about bad outcomes." Others were coded as *D*-statements – ones that emphasize a civic duty to vote. We coded others as *m*, or mobilization statements; these were ones that tried to persuade voters to go to the polls. Ones that we coded as *m*-statements frequently included the word "you," as in "you pick up the ballot" or "you vote."

On average, 88% of the 1,266 fall into the category of *B*-statements, with a range across speeches from 78% to 98%.[4] The results point to an even

---

[4] For this analysis we and our research assistants read the speeches and identified the arguments (or *debate points*) in each speech. Next we assigned each argument to one of 12 predefined types of phrases. Each of the 12 types of statements, in turn, was classified as one of the three types of statements – *B*, *m*, or *D*. To check for intercoder reliability, we used an automated content analysis software program, *ReadMe* (King et al. 2010). *ReadMe* takes as input a set of text documents, a categorization scheme chosen by the user, and a small subset of hand-classified text documents and assigns additional, uncoded documents into these same categories. We provided 250 coded arguments as an input to *ReadMe* to predict the allocation of the remaining 1,016

greater prevalence of B-statements if they are weighed by the number of words dedicated to these statements (or, equivalently, by the amount of time taken up by them in the speech). Calculated this way, a mere 5% are m-statements. Almost never did presidential candidates emphasize a duty to vote. We did find a few statements (3% of the total) that tried to trigger a sense of partisanship, presumably with the aim of mobilizing people who have strong party identities.

Of course, one might expect candidates at such a high level to spend much of their rhetorical energy trying to get people to choose them over their opponents, and to leave the work of mobilization to party activists. What's more, to the extent that people are inculcated with a norm that says it's their duty to vote, they may not need to be reminded of this duty by candidates. Yet, given the importance of turnout to the outcome of presidential races, it is hard to reconcile the 5-to-88% mix of m- to B-statements, and the near-absence of statements about normative obligations to vote, with the idea that differential utilities play no role in mobilization.

Higher turnout in high-stake elections; interest in politics trumping income, education, and other factors in explaining individual turnout; and candidates' overwhelming rhetorical emphasis on the reasons why it will be better for voters if they prevail over rivals: all of these should lead us to reconsider whether people's calculus of voting gives near-zero weight to B.

Close Elections and Turnout

In most democracies, the smaller on average the margin of victory between the winner and the first loser, the higher the turnout rate (Cox and Munger 1989, Blais 2000). A common interpretation of the close-election effect is that people are responding to the increasing probability that their vote will be pivotal. Some authors find in this response a rational reaction to real changes in probabilities. But they probably should not: the shift from one highly improbable event to another one, even if the latter is less improbable, shouldn't produce a behavioral difference among voters who have a firm grasp of the magnitude of these probabilities. Schwartz (1987: 118) made the fallacy vivid: "saying that closeness increases the probability of being pivotal ... is like saying that tall men are more likely than short men to bump their heads on the moon."

As a first step toward evaluating the impact of close races it is worth considering whether, in general, voters overestimate the probability of casting a tie-breaking vote. In a study of students at two Canadian universities, Blais (2000) found that about 10 to 15 percent of respondents overestimate p. Our own research results are in line with his conclusions: large majorities of individuals are aware that the probability of casting a decisive vote is very small, though a minority does overestimate this subjective probability.

---

arguments into the categories. The coding decisions of human coders and the *ReadMe* program were correlated at 0.98.

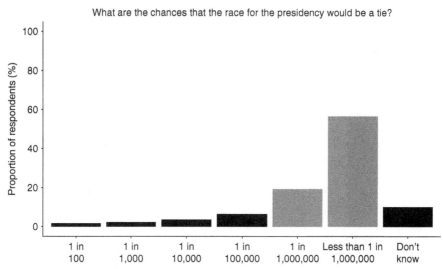

What are the chances that the race for the presidency would be a tie?

FIGURE 3.2 Respondents' assessments of chances for a presidential tie in the United States.
Source: Authors' survey.

We studied perceptions of p in a 2013 online convenience survey.[5] We asked respondents to assess the chances that a race for the US presidency would be a tie so that one additional vote would make the difference between who wins and who loses. We asked them to indicate whether the chances were one in: one hundred, one thousand, ten thousand, one hundred thousand, one million, or less than one in a million. The modal answer was the technically correct one: less than one in a million. About 76% responded that the chances were one in a million or less (Figure 3.2). Only about 14% of respondents much overestimated the chances of a tie, with 7% considering these chances as one in a hundred thousand and another 7% as one in ten thousand or greater. About 10% of our respondents did not provide an estimate.

Whatever people's perceptions of the size of p, what role do these perceptions play in their turnout decisions? Thalheimer (1995) asked 125 students at the University of Montreal whether they would vote in an upcoming referendum on Quebec sovereignty if they were certain that their vote would make no difference in the result.[6] Only seven percent of them said they would not, suggesting that p was not an important consideration for the remaining 93 percent. Blais and Young (1996) replicated Thalheimer's study, among representative samples, ahead of a referendum in Quebec and a general election in British Columbia. They reported comparable figures of four and nine percent,

---

[5] This survey was conducted in late spring–early summer of 2013 with 1,016 respondents recruited through Amazon.com's Mechanical Turk.

[6] Thalheimer (1995) as described by Blais (2000), pp. 70–1.

respectively, who said that they would abstain if they were absolutely sure there was no chance their vote could not make a difference.[7] In multivariate analyses of the decision to vote among Blais's Canadian samples, overestimates of p are not associated with a greater likelihood of turning out to vote.[8] Hence, if only people who thought they might cast a tie-breaking vote went to the polls, turnout would be a small fraction of its actual levels in most elections.

If most people do not grossly overestimate the chances of casting the tie-breaking vote in elections that are not especially close, do these estimates grow in close races? Are these perceptions responsible for close-election boosts to turnout? A field experiment conducted by Biggers and coauthors (2017) yields insights into this question. They conducted a field experiment in which they informed a treatment group that an upcoming race would be close. The group that received this message turned out at higher rates than those who did not. A follow-up survey experiment indicated that people who learned that the race would be close were more interested in voting and more likely to believe that their vote might be pivotal. But they were also more likely to believe that friends and family would look askance at them if they abstained, and reported increased expectations of feeling guilty if they stayed away from the polls. The authors concluded that election closeness affects individuals' extrinsic and intrinsic motivations to turn out to vote; its positive effect on turnout is "likely not isolated to increased perceptions that one's vote is pivotal" (p. 1). This conclusion is not far from Blais's (2000), that people "rely on the vague notion that their vote might count more in a close election rather than on an estimate of the probability that their vote could be decisive" (p. 78).

If the boost in turnout in close races cannot be fully explained by people believing they will cast the decisive vote, another natural interpretation is that campaigns and other agents of mobilization ratchet up their get-out-the-vote efforts when the outcome appears to be close. It is manifestly true that they do so. But the costly abstention model says that people are also more likely to vote on their own steam when the race is tight, even when not prodded by others, as we shall soon show.

The close-election effect emerges less regularly and robustly than the importance-of-election effect. One complication is that theory trains our attention on voters' perceptions of how close the eventual result appears to be at the moment when they decide whether to vote. But most measurement focuses on the outcome of the race, the perceptions of which are likely to be imperfect. In addition, the margin of victory is presumably a function in part of turnout, which – theory has it – is a function of how close it appears to be.

---

[7] Blais and Young (1996), as described by Blais (2000), p. 71.

[8] Blais (2000) reported that perceived closeness of the election is positively related with the decision to vote, though through an additive model of p and B, rather than the multiplicative term $(p)B$ as postulated in Riker and Ordeshook. This theoretical solution, however, creates some difficult problems. For instance, it implies that people who care almost nothing about who wins will nevertheless be enticed to vote for the pure sport of breaking a tie. The perceived closeness is also only weakly correlated with the subjective probability of breaking a tie.

Given this complex causal structure, it is useful to look at field experiments like the Biggers one just discussed. Another field experiment, one that failed to produce heightened turnout in a close race, is equally telling. Enos and Fowler (2013) took advantage of a tie in an election for the Massachusetts State House in the 6th Worcester district. Because of a tie, the race had to be rerun. Before the special election, the investigators contacted a randomly chosen group of registered voters. They were reminded of the tie and told that the special election was likely to be razor-close as well. Yet the treatment group's turnout rate was not significantly higher than that of a control group. It seems likely that this was a case in which γ was perceived as large but it was dragged down by a low B: many people saw little stake in who would represent them in the state legislature. The formulation in *The American Voter* again comes to mind: "the person who thinks the outcome is in doubt is more likely to vote if the intensity of his partisan preference is strong" (Campbell et al. 1960: 99).

OUR SURVEY-EXPERIMENTAL EVIDENCE

Observational evidence of the kind discussed earlier can be hard to interpret. Do apparently important elections attract more people to the polls because they care more about the outcome (high B)? Alternatively, could it be because these elections are covered heavily in the media and people are very aware of them, so that less cognitive effort is required of participants (low C)? Does turnout rise in highly competitive races (high γ) because would-be voters are more engaged and excited, or simply because campaigns intensify their get-out-the-vote efforts? We have posited that costs of abstention are intrinsic; but what if, as some have written, people are solely focused on extrinsic pressure and avoiding social blame? Perhaps, insulated from social pressure, they would feel free to abstain.

Building on the observational evidence just reviewed, in the remainder of this chapter we turn to a series of survey experiments. Doing so helps us to identify causal effects proposed in the costly abstention theory of electoral participation. In the survey experiments reported here, we expose respondents to distinct treatments – vignettes asking them to think about candidates or election outcomes in distinct ways – and then ask how they would behave or react. Random assignment of a sufficiently large number of survey respondents ensures that those in the distinct treatment and control groups will be similar in all the relevant ways, on average; so any differences (beyond sampling error) that we observe in their answers, posttreatment, can be interpreted as a reaction to the treatment itself, not to some preexisting difference among them. The main disadvantage of the survey experiments is that people are asked to react to hypothetical situations. We therefore view our results as a complement to the real-world observational data and the field experiments discussed earlier.

To recruit participants in our survey experiments reviewed in this chapter, we turned to Amazon's Mechanical Turk (www.mturk.com). Mechanical Turk is an online, web-based platform for recruiting and paying subjects to perform simple tasks. It offers a novel subject pool and has emerged as a promising tool for conducting experimental research in the social sciences (Berinsky et al. 2012, Huber et al. 2012, and Healy and Lenz 2014). A drawback is that these are convenience samples, not representative ones. Nevertheless, Berinsky and coauthors (2012) indicated that Mechanical Turk samples are more diverse than typical experimental samples and not substantially different on many demographic and political variables from nationally representative samples in the United States. Additionally, they showed that estimates of average treatment effects are similar in Mechanical Turk and original samples when they replicate published experimental studies of convenience and nationally representative samples on Mechanical Turk (see Coppock forthcoming as well). To address concerns about the generalizability of our results to the US population, we applied poststratification weights based on available demographic data to our samples (Franco et al. 2017). The results of the experiments are substantively identical across the weighted and unweighted data.[9]

Importance and Closeness: The Turnout Experiment

We focus first on the impact of election importance and expected closeness on individuals' propensity to vote. Our theoretical framework generates the following testable hypotheses:

Hypothesis 1 The more a person cares about the outcome of an election – the greater her differential utility benefits over outcomes – the more likely she is to vote.[10]

Hypothesis 2 When people view elections as highly competitive – the margin of victory will be small – they are more likely to turn out; but only when they also view the election as important. A close race in what they view as an unimportant election will not increase their propensity to vote.

To test these hypotheses, we recruited 1,020 US adults to respond to a survey, which included a *turnout* experiment.[11] We asked each participant

---

[9] More details about the application of poststratification weights and results are reported in the appendix.

[10] Formally, with regards to the rewards from voting, $\frac{\delta P}{\delta B} > 0$. By contrast, in the Riker–Ordeshook framework, and implicitly in those emphasizing the private benefits of voting, B enters into the utility calculation of voters only through the product $(p)B$. It follows that when p is close to zero, as in a typical race, $(p)B$ is close to zero as well, independent of how large B is. In this case $\frac{\delta P}{\delta B} \approx 0$.

[11] The survey was fielded in March–April 2016. The original sample included 1,162 respondents and we have eliminated about 12 percent of them because they could not pass two attention

to read a short vignette about a hypothetical election scenario. Respondents were randomly assigned to one of four vignettes; these were the treatments.[12] The vignettes were designed to manipulate two dimensions of our theory: the differential benefit a person derives from his or her favored candidate being elected, B, and the closeness of the result, γ. Hence there were four treatments: *Important, Close*; *Important, Not close*; *Unimportant, Close*; and *Unimportant, Not close*.

Box 3.1. The *Turnout* experiment

Question. Do the importance and closeness of an election increase participation?

Participants. 1,020 adult US residents recruited through the *Mechanical Turk* in March/April 2016.

Key finding 1. Participants are more likely to vote when the election is important, regardless of whether the result is likely to be close or lopsided.

Key finding 2. Participants are more likely to vote when the election is close, but only if it is also important.

We designed the survey so that we would be able to experimentally manipulate importance and closeness in isolation from potential confounding effects, such as intensified media coverage or party mobilization in important and close races. If in reality higher turnout were due to these other extrinsic and cost-lowering effects of important and close races, then we should not see higher (hypothetical) turnout in this treatment.

Respondents in the *Important, Close* treatment were presented with the following script:

Imagine an election for governor is coming up in your state. Keep in mind that the governor has significant control over the state budget and taxes, and she or he can implement policies that would bring new jobs. Therefore whom we choose to elect as governor can have a big impact on our everyday lives.

You believe that candidate A, your favored one, would handle the position of governor very well but the opponent, candidate B, will handle it very badly.

Reliable polls reported in the media indicate that the race is very close.

The first two paragraphs are designed to instill a sense of importance about the (hypothetical) gubernatorial election to respondents by highlighting

---

checks we included in the survey, a common practice in online surveys. Descriptive statistics about the sample are presented in the appendix.

[12] A likelihood ratio test from the multinomial logit regression of treatment assignment on the observable characteristics of respondents (gender, age, education, employment status, partisanship) is statistically insignificant (Wald $\chi^2_{(15)} = 8.68$, $p < 0.89$), suggesting that random assignment was successful.

powerful capacities of the governor and by stating that the respondent has a clear preference for one of the candidates over the other. Together, the statements suggests a high B. The last sentence indicates that the race is highly competitive, suggesting a high γ.

In a second treatment, *Important, Not close*, we change the last sentence to signal a race that was uncompetitive (low γ):

> Imagine an election for governor is coming up in your state. Keep in mind that the governor has significant control over the state budget and taxes, and she or he can implement policies that would bring new jobs. Therefore whom we choose to elect as governor can have a big impact on our everyday lives.
>
> You believe that candidate A, your favored one, would handle the position of governor very well but the opponent, candidate B, will handle it very badly.
>
> Reliable polls reported in the media indicate that it's pretty clear which candidate is going to win.

The third and fourth treatments repeat the close/lopsided pattern but downplay the importance of the election outcome to the voter, so that B approaches zero. We do this by dropping any mention of important functions of governors and by asking the respondent to consider two candidates whom he or she expects to do an equally good job in office. The vignette for the *Unimportant, Close* treatment reads as follows:

> Imagine an election for governor is coming up in your state.
>
> You favor candidate A but believe that the opponent, candidate B, would probably also do a good job.
>
> Reliable polls reported in the media indicate that the race is very close.

Finally, the vignette for the *Unimportant, Not close* treatment is:

> Imagine an election for governor is coming up in your state.
>
> You favor candidate A but believe that the opponent, candidate B, would probably also do a good job.
>
> Reliable polls reported in the media indicate that it's pretty clear which candidate is going to win.

This experimental setup results in a 2×2 design, as shown in Table 3.1.

To check whether our manipulations of B worked as intended, we asked our respondents, in a posttreatment question, how important gubernatorial elections are in their state. On average, respondents in *Important* treatments (1 and 2) viewed them as more important than did those in the *Unimportant* treatments (3 and 4). The differences are statistically significant.[13] Thus, the importance manipulations were effective.

---

[13] The answer options ran from "not important at all" (coded 1) to "extremely important" (coded 5). The means of responses were 4.14 and 4.12, respectively, in treatments 1 and 2, and 3.74 and 3.67, respectively, in treatments 3 and 4.

TABLE 3.1 *Setup of the* Turnout *experiment*

	$\gamma > 0$	$\gamma \approx 0$
$B > 0$	Important, Close (Treatment 1)	Important, Not close (Treatment 2)
$B \approx 0$	Unimportant, Close (Treatment 3)	Unimportant, Not close (Treatment 4)

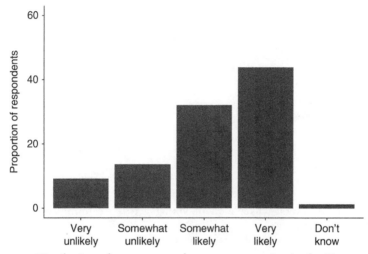

FIGURE 3.3 Distribution of responses to the outcome question in the *Turnout* experiment.
Source: Authors' survey.

The outcome we were interested in was the stated likelihood of voting, and was the same for all treatments:

Imagine that on the day of the election you have important personal matters to attend to, and it will not be easy for you to turn out to vote (balloting is secret).
How likely would you be to turn out to vote anyway?

Answer choices were *very unlikely, somewhat unlikely, somewhat likely,* and *very likely,* which we coded on a scale of 1 to 4, respectively. We attributed costs to voting (*"it will not be easy for you to turn out to vote"*) so as not to render the participant's turnout decision trivial. To rule out expectations of private payoffs and social sanctions, we indicated that balloting is secret.

Given that our outcome question is on the self-reported likelihood of voting in a hypothetical election, we expected a large percentage of the respondents to answer affirmatively. Indeed, about 44% of our respondents said that they would be very likely to turn out to vote (Figure 3.3). Still, there is a significant

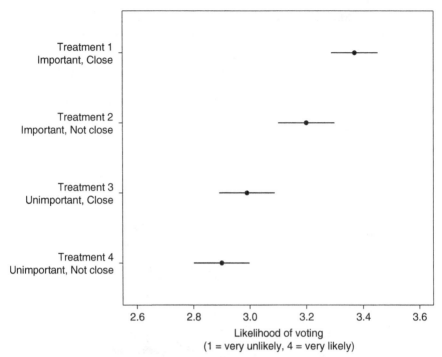

FIGURE 3.4 The average likelihood of voting across treatment conditions in the *Turnout* experiment.
Note: Horizontal lines correspond to 95% confidence intervals. *Source:* Authors' survey.

variation in responses: about 32% said it was somewhat likely, and about a quarter of respondents (23%) said they would be very unlikely or somewhat unlikely to turn out to vote.

Respondents are more likely to vote when the election is close, but only if it is also important (see Figure 3.4, which reports the average likelihood of voting across the treatments). In the first two treatments, both of which featured important elections, turnout is higher in the close election (treatment 1) than in the lopsided one (treatment 2). The difference in average turnout between treatments 1 and 2 is statistically significant. But when the election outcome was unimportant (treatments 3 and 4), the closeness of the election had no effect on the likelihood of voting.[14]

Respondents are also more likely to vote when the election is important, and this effect held in close *and* lopsided elections. The impact of exogenous

[14] On the 1–5 scale, the average turnout in treatment 1 was 3.37, in treatment 2, 3.20; this difference is statistically significant ($p < 0.05$). In contrast, the difference in the average likelihood of voting between treatments 3 and 4 is not statistically significant ($p = 0.34$). Note that since our treatments involve manipulations across two dimensions (importance and closeness), we do not use interactions.

changes in *B* can be seen by comparing the treatment pairs 1–3 (both close) and 2–4 (both lopsided) in Figure 3.4. Turnout was significantly higher in treatment 1 than in treatment 3, and in treatment 2 than in treatment 4. In other words, holding competitiveness constant, the importance of the contest always makes a difference.[15] Furthermore, the magnitude of the effect was larger for *B* than for γ: how much a person cared about who would win mattered more than how close the election was likely to be.

These results provide support for the costly abstention model, specifically for Hypotheses 1 and 2. Close elections encourage turnout, but only when the election is viewed as important. Whether the result is likely to be close or lopsided, important elections boost people's willingness to vote. The findings weigh against a rival, mobilization story, whereby higher turnout in important and close elections reflects elite actors' stimulating people to go to the polls. Our experimental design did not feature greater elite inducements or heavier advertising. Nevertheless, people responded.

The Abstention *Experiment*

Our core theoretical conjecture is that abstaining – or anticipating abstaining – when one cares about the outcome of an election induces unpleasant psychic tensions (high costs of abstention), and a drive to avoid these tensions lies behind many people's decisions to participate. These tensions mount higher still with the excitement and urgency of a tight race. The next step in our empirical strategy is to try to get closer to this subjective mechanism. We are interested both in whether abstention generates internalized dissonance and, if so, how this effect compares with any extrinsic social pressure that people might experience if they abstain.

To test this conjecture we need a measure of unpleasant psychic tensions, or internalized dissonance, that a person might experience, and we need to distinguish internalized dissonance from the effects of social pressure. We turn to the psychological concept of *negative affect*. Watson et al. (1988: 1063) wrote that negative affect "is a general dimension of subjective distress and unpleasurable engagement that subsumes a variety of aversive mood states." These mood states include anger, distress, and nervousness; the stress they reflect is related to intrinsic costs of abstention as we conceive them. In turn, emotions like guilt and shame are linked to extrinsic social pressure, which one might also experience when anticipating abstention. Hence our empirical strategy is to present subjects with the possibility of abstention and measure induced levels of intrinsic and extrinsic negative affects.

---

[15] Recall that closeness was indicated with the phrase, "reliable polls in the media indicate that the race is very close." In the *close*-election treatments, the average likelihood of voting when the election was also important was 3.37 (treatment 1); it was 2.99 when the election was unimportant (treatment 3). The difference is highly significant ($p < 0.001$). In the *not close* elections, the average likelihood of voting was 3.20 when the election was important (2) and 2.90 when it was not (treatment 4). Again, the difference is highly significant ($p < 0.001$).

Our second, *abstention* experiment measures the impact of hypothetical abstention on experimental subjects' moods, or affect. The goal is to look for signs of internal dissonance and social pressure in the context of elections of varying importance. We test the following hypotheses:

Hypothesis 3 When people contemplate abstaining in important elections they experience internal dissonance, a deterioration in their subjective mood; contemplation of abstaining in unimportant elections has no such effect.

Hypothesis 4 These mood effects are intensified when the outcome appears close.

Hypothesis 5 Abstention effects on turnout are due in part to internalized dissonance, not entirely – and not principally – to extrinsic, social effects.

The last is one key distinction between our theory and social network theories.

Box 3.2. The *Abstention* experiment

Question. Do people experience negative affect when they contemplate abstaining in important elections, and is the affect linked to intrinsic or extrinsic considerations?

Participants. 1,020 adult US residents recruited through the *Mechanical Turk* in March/April 2016.

Key finding 1. Participants report significantly higher levels of negative affect when anticipating not voting in an important election than in an unimportant one.

Key finding 2. Negative affect spurred by abstention is amplified when the election outcome is close.

Key finding 3. Abstention-related negative affect is *not* mainly sparked by extrinsic, social considerations.

Recall that in the turnout experiment we assigned respondents, randomly, to one of four election scenarios: *Important, Close*; *Important, Not close*; *Unimportant, Close*; and *Unimportant, Not close*. The outcome question was whether the respondent would turn out to vote. The abstention experiment followed immediately after this outcome question, with the same sample of respondents. They were randomly assigned to one of four groups (Table 3.2). We asked respondents in each group to imagine that they were not able to vote in the hypothetical election described in the turnout experiment; an unforeseen event would keep them from the polls. Some treatments then added that they would later come into contact with friends or neighbors after the election and their nonparticipation would be discussed. The idea is to induce

TABLE 3.2 *Treatment vignettes in the* Abstention *experiment*

Treatment	Vignette
Intrinsic	Now imagine that when Election Day comes, it turns out to be a complicated day for you and you are not able to vote.
Extrinsic–Friends	Now imagine that when Election Day comes, it turns out to be a complicated day for you and you are not able to vote.
	You meet a group of friends the next day and the topic of the election comes up. You explain that you were not able to get to the polls.
Extrinsic–Neighbors	Now imagine that when Election Day comes, it turns out to be a complicated day for you and you are not able to vote.
	You meet a group of neighbors the next day and the topic of the election comes up. You explain that you were not able to get to the polls.
Extrinsic–Friends (alt. version)	Now imagine that when Election Day comes, it turns out to be a complicated day for you and you are not able to vote.
	You meet a group of friends the next day and the topic of the election comes up. You tell them you did not vote.

(hypothetical) abstention and then observe whether internal dissonance and external shame mount, and to see whether it mounts more in cases of important and close elections than in unimportant and lopsided ones. Our design also allows us to compare the impact of induced abstention on a person's mood when abstention remains a private event versus when it becomes publicized to friends and acquaintances.

In the first treatment, *Intrinsic*, respondents were asked to imagine that they are unexpectedly not able to vote. In the second and third treatments, *Extrinsic–Friends* and *Extrinsic–Neighbors*, we repeated the same vignette but also asked respondents to imagine that they meet a group of friends or neighbors after the election and tell them that they were not able to vote. The fourth treatment, *Extrinsic–Friends (alt. version)*, considered a variation in the wording of the second treatment: instead of imagining explaining to a group of friends that she was "not able to get to the polls," the respondent was asked to imagine that she simply tells them that she "did not vote." The purpose of these last three treatments was to explore the effects, if any, of extrinsic considerations on respondents' moods.[16]

---

[16] We experimented with different wording in the social-impact treatments, in part because we wanted to be sure that the wording alone was not leading us to underestimate the response.

The key outcome of interest is subjective dissonance. As mentioned, we measure this dissonance with the respondents' self-reported negative affect. We use a tool developed by Watson et al. (1988) that is widely used by psychologists: the Positive and Negative Affect Schedule (PANAS).[17] PANAS is a 20-item self-reported measure of two dominant dimensions of emotional experience, Positive Affect (PA) and Negative Affect (NA). High PA is a state of high energy and pleasurable engagement, low PA of lethargy and sadness. High NA is a state of distress and unpleasurable engagement, low NA a state of calm and serenity. Watson and his coauthors report that these two dimensions consistently emerge in studies of affective structure, both in the United States and in several other countries. In the implementation of PANAS, respondents are asked to rate the extent to which they experience each of the ten mood states in the PA scale and another ten in the NA scale.[18] The points of the scale are labeled *very slightly or not at all, a little, moderately, quite a bit*, and *very much*, coded from 1 to 5, respectively.

We asked our respondents to complete an abbreviated PANAS scale with the question: "Indicate to what extent you would imagine yourself feeling these negative emotions after the hypothetical Election Day just described." Given our theoretical focus on costs of abstention, we are interested in negative affect emotions. We included seven relevant mood states: *distressed, upset, guilty, ashamed, nervous, afraid* and *angry*.[19] We also probed two positive affect mood states, *interested* and *active*. Doing so allowed us to see whether our treatments had an impact on respondents' positive affect, which we did not expect.

A clear pattern emerges. When told they would abstain, respondents in the *Important* election treatments (treatments 1 and 2) scored significantly higher on negative affect than respondents in the *Unimportant* treatments (treatments 3 and 4; see Figure 3.5). Those in the *Important* election treatments felt especially distressed, upset, and guilty. They also displayed elevated levels of anger and shame, but to a lesser degree. The mean levels of all of these emotions were

---

Hence, for instance, the strong and explicit formulation in the *Friends – alternative version* vignette, "you tell them you did not vote."

[17] The 1988 paper by Watson and his coauthors has been cited more than 28,000 times as of February 2018 according to Google Scholar. Studies using representative and convenience samples in a variety of national contexts have confirmed PANAS as a reliable and valid measure – e.g., Terracciano et al. (2003) for an application in Italy, and Crawford and Henry (2004) in the United Kingdom. It has been used in political science research as well, for instance, by Arceneaux (2012) and by Waismel-Manor et al. (2011).

[18] The PA scale consists of the following 10 mood states: *attentive, interested, alert, excited, enthusiastic, inspired, proud, determined, strong,* and *active*. The 10 mood states that comprise the NA scale are: *distressed, upset, guilty, scared, hostile, irritable (angry), ashamed, nervous, jittery,* and *afraid (fearful)*.

[19] We decided to leave out the remaining three emotions in the original PANAS NA scale (*scared, jittery, hostile*) because either they were too close in meaning to those we already measure or were not so relevant given the context of study.

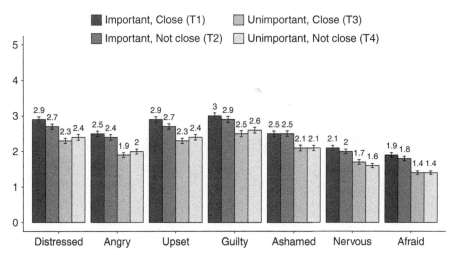

FIGURE 3.5 Negative affect emotions across experimental groups in the *Abstention* experiment.
Note: Vertical lines correspond to 95% confidence intervals. *Source:* Authors' survey.

higher in the *Important* election treatments than in the *Unimportant* ones; the differences are statistically significant.[20] We also see a trend toward closeness of the election leading to more negative mood states under induced abstention when the election is important (comparison of treatments 1 and 2), though the effects do not quite reach conventional significance levels. The treatments did not result in statistically significant differences on positive moods (*interested* and *active*, not shown in the figures) across the experimental groups.

Are emotional reactions to being kept from the polls driven by intrinsic tensions: a subjective dissonance felt when one cares about the outcome of an election *and* anticipates not voting? Alternatively, it could be by extrinsic ones: concern about what friends and neighbors will think if the person fails to participate, especially in an important election? The abstention experiment allows us to answer this question, as we randomly assigned our respondents to treatments highlighting intrinsic and extrinsic considerations (recall Table 3.2).

In fact we find no evidence that abstainers' dissonance is driven mainly by extrinsic considerations, as network mobilization theories predict. Figure 3.6 reports the mean levels of negative emotions across the groups in the abstention experiment for respondents who were assigned to the *Important, Close* treatment in the turnout experiment. In none of the three treatments that

[20] The differences in average responses between *Important* and *Unimportant* election treatments are statistically significant ($p < 0.05$) for all emotions considered. These comparisons are between treatments 1–3 and treatments 2–4. Recall that respondents were asked to rate to what extent they would imagine themselves feeling these emotions in a scale from 1 (*very slightly or not at all*) to 5 (*extremely*).

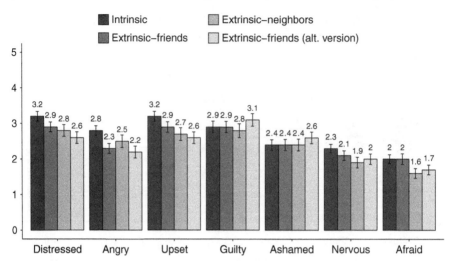

FIGURE 3.6 Negative affect emotions across experimental groups in the (*Important, Close*) election group of the *Abstention* experiment.
Note: Vertical lines correspond to 95% confidence intervals. *Source:* Authors' survey.

asked people to imagine reporting their absence from the polls to acquaintances did subjects evince more anger, upset, or nervousness (or other negative affect emotions) than in the treatment without social pressure. In fact, the evidence points in the other direction: intrinsic considerations more powerfully stir negative affect emotions. For five of the seven emotions (*distressed, angry, upset, nervous, afraid*) the mean levels of negative affect emotions are statistically higher in the *intrinsic* group than at least one of the extrinsic treatment groups. Shame and guilt, natural responses to social pressure, trend higher in the extrinsic treatments. The results are similar for the remaining three treatment groups of the turnout experiment.

To summarize, our abstention survey experiment provides strong support for the theorized link between abstention and subjective costs. Our theory of costly abstention posits that when an election outcome seems important to a person, the prospect of abstention causes her to experience dissonance – an unpleasant drive state – even when she is aware that her participation would not change the outcome. This is exactly what we observed. Our experimental subjects reported feeling significantly more distressed and upset when they considered abstaining in such an election than when they considered abstaining in an unimportant election. We have discerned support for Hypotheses 3, that important elections drive up the psychic costs of abstention, and weaker, but suggestive, evidence in support of Hypothesis 4, that dissonance is amplified when the race is also close. We find strong evidence in favor of Hypothesis 5: that intrinsic dissonance is at least as powerful a component of costly abstention as is social pressures from friends or neighbors.

Civic Duty: Unconditional or Influenced by B?

Riker and Ordeshook solved the paradox of voting by stipulating that people feel a moral obligation to vote; they derive positive utility from "compliance with the ethic of voting" (1968: 28). That a sense of civic duty does play a role in turning people out receives support from Blais et al. (2000: 193). They conclude, in a study of two Canadian elections, that "the sense of duty ... clearly is the most compelling motivation to go to the polls." As Riker and Ordeshook conceptualized it, duty was a trait that adhered to individuals; its force might vary from person to person but not from election to election. By contrast, rule utilitarians view norms around voting as conditional: one may have a duty to vote or to stay home, depending on the importance of the election and on the expected margin of victory of the winner over the loser. Thought of this way, norms about electoral participation seem closer to the subjective imperatives that we are calling costs of abstention.[21]

In this section we explore the power of moral obligations to get people to the polls; the relative effectiveness of duty versus importance-of-election factors; and whether the perceived importance of an election shapes how strongly people feel a duty to vote. Our strategy is to experimentally manipulate respondents' perception of the importance of an upcoming election and the salience to them of a duty to vote, with the outcome of interest being their stated intention to vote in upcoming elections. We conducted the *duty* experiment in August, 2014, with a sample of 504 adults. We took advantage of the proximity of gubernatorial elections, which were scheduled to take place in 30 US states in November 2014, and recruited respondents exclusively from these 30 states using Mechanical Turk. We randomly assigned respondents to one of four treatments – four distinct vignettes about the November election (Table 3.3).[22] After the vignettes, we asked about the importance of the election, about respondents' perceptions of the duty to vote, and about their intention to turn out.

---

[21] Galais and Blais (2014a) offer evidence of some effects of economic states on people's sense of duty. In the wake of the Great Recession in Spain, young people who suffered a loss of income, lost their mortgages, and were at risk of eviction from their homes experienced a decline in their sense of duty to participate in elections.

[22] Hence, unlike the previous two experiments, here our reference is a real election. The survey was open only to residents of US states where a gubernatorial election was going to be held. A likelihood ratio test from the multinomial logit regression of treatment assignment on gender, age, education level, and employment status is statistically insignificant (Wald $\chi^2_{(12)} = 15.51$, $p < 0.21$). See the appendix for the descriptives of the sample.

TABLE 3.3 *Experimental conditions and vignettes in the* Duty *experiment*

Control	The 2014 [STATE] gubernatorial election will take place on November 4.
B	The 2014 [STATE] gubernatorial election will take place on November 4. Who we choose to elect as the Governor of [STATE] will have a big impact on our everyday lives. Please remember that the Governor can • have significant control over the state budget and taxes • implement policies that can bring new jobs to [STATE] • expand the scope and improve the quality of social services and health care
D	The 2014 [STATE] gubernatorial election will take place on November 4. Many people think that every citizen has a civic duty or moral obligation to vote in elections.
DD	The 2014 [STATE] gubernatorial election will take place on November 4. Please remember that • the whole point of democracy is that citizens are active participants, that we have a voice in government through our vote • democracy depends on the participation of the citizens in elections • the right to vote is a duty as well as a privilege

---

> **Box 3.3. The *Duty* experiment**
>
> ***Questions.*** How does civic duty compare to the importance of an election in mobilizing people to vote? Is civic duty an unconditional norm?
>
> ***Participants.*** 504 adult US residents recruited through the *Mechanical Turk* in August 2014.
>
> ***Key finding 1.*** Reminding participants of the importance of an election increased their intention to vote; no such effect is observed when they were reminded of their civic duty.
>
> ***Key finding 2.*** Participants' sense of civic duty is influenced by the stakes of an election.

Subjects in the *B*-treatment read a list of the powers that governors and reminders that a governor's decisions can have a big impact on everyday lives of people in the state. We also included two duty conditions, at different "dosages." The *D-treatment* stated that "many people think that every citizen has a duty or moral obligation to vote." The *DD-treatment* did the same, but offered a series of arguments for why it is a person's civic duty to vote. Hence the appeal is to any internalized norm to vote – we are studying the intrinsic component of civic duty, D_I (Gerber et al. 2008). Subjects in the control

TABLE 3.4 *Manipulation checks for the* Duty *experiment*

Treatment condition	Subjective importance of the election (1=not at all important, 5=very important)	Perception of civic duty (0=none, 2=a lot)
Control	4.04	0.89
B	4.34**	1.07*
D	4.22	1.04
DD	4.03	1.08**

Note: The question for measuring the subjective importance of the election was: "How important do you think it is which candidate wins the upcoming gubernatorial election and is the governor of [STATE] in the next term?" The question for measuring perception of civic duty was: "If you were not to vote in an election, would you feel that you neglected your duty as a citizen?" Stars indicate statistically significant differences in average responses with the control condition: $*p < 0.1$, $**p < 0.05$. *Source*: Authors' survey.

condition were simply reminded that a gubernatorial election would take place in their state.

Our vignettes succeeded in manipulating respondents' subjective sense of the importance of the election and their perceptions of a civic duty to vote (Table 3.4). We asked them how important it was that their preferred candidate wins the gubernatorial election. Those in the *B*-treatment saw the election as more important than did subjects in the control; the difference was statistically significant ($p < 0.05$). Turning to manipulations of the civic duty to vote, people needed a heavy dose to respond. The *DD-treatment* heightened their sense of civic duty: subjects in this condition were more likely than those in the control to say that they would neglect their duty as a citizen if they did not vote. Average responses to this question of people in the *D-treatment* group were not statistically different from those in the control group.

In line with our expectations, subjects who were primed to see the election as important had a heightened sense of civic duty as well, even though the *B*-treatment said nothing about duty (Table 3.4, column 3). But the opposite was not true – subjects who were primed to keep in mind their civic duty did *not* see the election as more important. Hence, people's sense of civic duty appears to be partially driven by how much they view as at stake in an election. This result increases our confidence in conceptualizing internalized civic duty, D_I, as part of costs of abstention, and suggests that the findings in the literature linking a higher sense of civic duty to increased participation might be due to people voting at higher rates in important elections (as we have seen) and then interpreting their actions as a reflection of their sense of duty.[23] Further research will be required to sort out the relationship between civic duty and *B*.

---

[23] See Galais and Blais (2014b) for evidence from two panel surveys, one in Canada and the other in Spain, that people's sense of duty was a motivator for participation.

TABLE 3.5 *Average treatment effects in the* Duty *experiment*

Outcome variable: Likelihood of voting	(1)		(2)	
	Coefficient	SE	Coefficient	SE
Importance (B)	0.29*	(0.14)	0.27*	(0.13)
Civic duty (D)	0.09	(0.14)	0.06	(0.13)
Civic duty (stronger $- DD$)	0.01	(0.14)	−0.004	(0.13)
Female			0.05	(0.10)
Age			0.02**	(0.004)
Education			0.11**	(0.04)
Employed			0.14	(0.10)
Constant	2.96**	(0.10)	1.85**	(0.20)
Observations	492		491	

Note: Ordinary least squares (OLS) regressions with robust standard errors in parentheses.
*$p < 0.05$, **$p < 0.01$. *Source*: Authors' survey.

Did the importance-of-outcome (B) and duty (D and DD) treatments influence subjects' propensity to vote? In fact, only the subjects in the B-treatment were more likely to vote than those in the control group. We learn this from regressing their responses to the posttreatment question, *How likely are you to vote in the upcoming gubernatorial election*, on their treatment assignment (see Table 3.5).[24] By contrast, subjects in the D- and DD-treatments were no more likely than those in the control to say they would vote.

Thus, in our duty experiment, framing the election as important had a larger effect than reminding people of their civic duty in boosting their intentions to turn out. This result does not imply that civic duty is irrelevant for turnout. People in the control group who evinced a strong sense of civic duty in the manipulation-check question were more likely to say they planned to vote. Still, the results argue for more research on the relative impact of B and civic duty on turnout, and hint that the former may be more powerful than the latter. Recall that in the calculus-of-voting models, just the opposite was true: the effect of B is insignificant and duty is crucial. In addition, our results argue against conceptualizing civic duty as an unconditional norm, and in favor of thinking about it as a B-sensitive cost of abstention.

Comparing Costly Abstention and Rule Utilitarianism

Costly abstention and rule-utilitarian models make several common predictions. Both predict that, other things being equal, turnout will rise when people view an election as important. Both propose that people view the strategic

---

[24] Respondents were given four choices of answer, from very unlikely (coded as 1) to very likely (coded as 4). Whereas the average likelihood of voting was 2.96 in the control group, it rose to 3.25 for subjects in the B-treatment, a statistically significant difference ($p < 0.05$).

TABLE 3.6 *Views on civic duty versus duty to abstain*

Do you agree or disagree with the following statements?				
Strongly agree	Agree	Neither agree nor disagree	Disagree	Strongly disagree
It is every citizen's duty to vote in an election				
30%	38%	15%	11%	6%
In order to preserve democracy, it is essential that the great majority of citizens vote				
36%	38%	13%	7%	5%
If a person doesn't care how an election comes out, then the person shouldn't vote				
16%	29%	25%	16%	13%
Citizens have a duty to abstain from voting when it takes too much effort to vote				
2%	7%	19%	28%	40%

Note: $N = 504$. Subjects are US residents recruited through Mechanical Turk in August 2014.

context of elections – who is likely to win and by how large a margin – from a supraindividual vantage point. But they also diverge in several respects. A key difference, as laid out in Chapter 2, is that rule-utilitarians' citizens also view the costs of participation from a supraindividual perspective and feel an obligation to minimize the social costs of voting – to minimize turnout – as long as the chances of the wrong candidate winning are not too large. There is no countervailing sense of widespread participation being a good thing. In our model, would-be voters pay attention to their own costs of participation, not social ones.

We noted earlier the discrepancy between normative democratic theory and rule utilitarianism on whether minimizing turnout (and hence the social costs of voting) is a desirable goal. Of course, for the purpose of explaining why citizens really do vote, what matters is not political philosophy but lay people's mindsets. Rule utilitarianism is a positive theory of why people turn out; if the factors it identifies as influencing the common person's decisions are not ones that common people are actually moved by, the theory is not successful. Our contention is that individuals' costs of voting, not their sense of a duty to abstain, weighs on their voting decisions. The results of a convenience-sample survey we conducted suggest that a duty to abstain is not a norm that many people share (Table 3.6). In the *duty* survey, we asked respondents their views about duties to vote and to abstain when voting is costly. Only nine percent agreed with the statement, "citizens have a duty to abstain from voting when it takes too much effort to vote." Not surprisingly, the idea that voting is a citizen's duty was roundly supported. About two-thirds agreed that "It is every citizen's duty to vote in an election"; three-quarters agreed that "In order to preserve democracy, it is essential that the great majority of citizens vote."

It is relevant to our own theory that respondents to the survey endorsed the idea that turnout is, and should be, driven in part by how much people care about who wins and who loses. Many were willing to give people who did not care about the result a pass on voting. Forty-five percent of our sample agreed that "if a person doesn't care how an election comes out, then the person shouldn't vote in it." In the notation of Riker and Ordeshook, low Bs seemed like a good reason to sit an election out.

To further explore the empirical validity of the rule-utilitarian models, we test one of its predictions, which derives from the citizens' assumed desire to minimize the social costs of voting. Recall that Feddersen and Sandroni (2006) divided ethical types according to whether they favored candidate 1 or 2. Assume that a majority supports candidate 2, a minority, candidate 1. It follows from their model that turnout will be higher among supporters of candidate 1, the minority side, than among the majority. The reason is that members of the majority wish to minimize the social costs of voting, so will reduce their level of turnout; whereas the minority will tolerate a higher social cost of voting to make up for their reduced probability of winning (Feddersen and Sandroni 2006, pp. 1276–7).

Box 3.4. The *Group turnout* experiment

Question. In a two-candidate election, is turnout higher among the supporters of the candidate expected to get smaller share of the votes, as rule utilitarianism predicts?

Participants. 1,020 adult US residents recruited through the *Mechanical Turk* in March/April 2016.

Key finding 1. No support is found for the rule-utilitarian model's prediction of higher minority turnout.

We tested this prediction by conducting a simple additional experiment among respondents who took part in the *turnout* and *abstention* experiments. We call this the *group turnout* experiment. Respondents were randomly assigned to one of two experimental groups, the *majority* and the *minority*. Majority group respondents read the following text:

Imagine that the November 2016 presidential election, between the Democratic and the Republican nominees, is forecast to be quite lopsided in your state.

Your party's candidate is expected to get around 65% of the votes and the other party's candidate to get about 35%.

Respondents assigned to the *minority* group received the same text but the expected vote shares were reversed: their preferred candidate was expected

TABLE 3.7 *Turnout among the majority and minority groups in the* Group turnout *experiment*

Treatment condition	N	Average effort to get to the polls (1=not hard at all, 5=very hard)
Majority group	514	3.69
Minority group	506	3.75

Source: Authors' survey.

to get 35 percent of the votes. The outcome question was the same for all respondents:

> Suppose that Election Day turns out to be a complicated day for you and it is hard to find time to get to the polls.
> How hard would you try to get to the polls? Please indicate on the scale below where 1 corresponds to "not hard at all" and 5 "very hard"?

Table 3.7 shows that respondents in the minority group are slightly more likely to turn out. But the difference is minuscule, basically not different from zero ($p = 0.51$). Thus we do not find support for rule-utilitarian models' prediction of higher minority turnout.

SUMMARY

We have tested a theory of electoral participation, the core idea of which is that people bear costs not just when they vote but also when they abstain. These costs grow in elections they view as important, more so if they also view them as close. The costs of abstention are intrinsic; even in the absence of being mobilized or anticipating social shame, abstention is costly.

We have offered the following experimental evidence in support of our theory from the *Turnout* and *Abstention* experiments:

- Induced increases in respondents' sense of the importance of elections – their utility differential over the outcome – increases their willingness to vote.
- Turnout propensities rise when the expected outcome of the race is close: people's stated willingness to vote is greater in competitive races, but only when the election's outcome matters to them.
- Exogenously imposed hypothetical abstention – being told that one did not vote – causes changes in subjective mood. Most importantly for our theory, only the combination of caring about an election outcome and abstaining leads people to experience significantly higher levels of negative affect – emotions like distress, anger, nervousness, and guilt.

We also offer preliminary evidence that the norm that people should vote, invoked by early rational choice theorists to explain positive turnout, is not static but instead conditional on the importance of an election in citizens' perceptions. Forgoing this duty, too, imposes costs of abstention. But the costs of abstention are not reducible to a conditional duty to vote. The relevant finding from the *Duty* experiment is:

- Focusing people on their duty to vote – D and DD in our experimental treatments – did not increase their stated intentions to participate in upcoming elections.

This should not be taken as evidence that the norm is irrelevant to voting propensities, since:

- People in the control condition who express a stronger sense of the duty to vote also express stronger intentions to vote in the upcoming elections.
- Focusing people's attention on the powers attached to the office to be filled (B – in this case, US governors) increases their intentions to vote; and a focus on these powers leads to an increase in people's sense of a duty to vote; that is, civic duty appears to be a function of B.

Finally, against rule-utilitarian theory, we demonstrated that few people recognize a duty to abstain in order to minimize the social costs of elections. Likewise, those who support the more popular side are not inclined to turn out at lower rates than those on the minority side. Together, these results cast doubt on the rule-utilitarian theory's key assumptions. Both the theory of costly abstention and rule utilitarianism generate predictions that accord with observed patterns in electoral turnout. But only the theory of costly abstention arrives at those predictions with realistic fundamental assumptions about political behavior.

APPENDIX

Descriptive Statistics of Mechanical Turk Samples

TABLE 3.8 Turnout, Abstention, *and* Group turnout *experiments – Sample descriptives*

Female (%)	43.5
Mean age	35.2
College graduate (%)	49.9
Full-time employed (%)	59.7
Democrat (%)	40.4
Republican (%)	15.7
N	1,020

TABLE 3.9 Duty *experiment – sample descriptives*

Female (%)	47.3
Mean age	33.9
College graduate (%)	47.9
Full-time employed (%)	47.8
Liberal/very liberal (%)	35.8
Conservative/very conservative (%)	11.6
N	504

Poststratification Weighting of the Samples

Our samples are younger and more educated on average than the overall US adult population, as it is often the case with Mechanical Turk samples (Berinsky et al. 2012). In order to address concerns about the generalizability of our experimental results to the broader US population, we applied poststratification weights to our samples and reanalyzed our experiments with weighted data. We have drawn on the 2016 Annual Social and Economic Supplement of the Current Population Survey of the US Census Bureau to calculate weights with respect to respondents' gender, age, and education levels. We have considered three age groups (between 18 and 34 years old, between 35 and 54 years old, and 55 years and above), two education categories (below 4-year college education and 4-year college education or above), and the gender (female and male) of respondents, resulting in 12 (3*2*2) exclusive groups of individuals. We have calculated weights for each of these 12 groups based on a comparison of their distribution in the US population and in our sample.

Figure 3.7 reports the average likelihood of voting across the treatments groups together for the unweighted (originally reported in Figure 3.4) and weighted data. We see that there is an overall increase in the likelihood of voting in the weighted results compared to the unweighted ones – this is expected, as with weighting the sample is adjusted to be older on average, and we know that likelihood of voting is positively correlated with age. But there is no change in the patterns we observe: in the weighted results, turnout is significantly higher in the close election (treatment 1) than in the lopsided one (treatment 2), but there is no such effect when election outcome was unimportant (treatments 3 and 4). Respondents were also more likely to vote when the election was important, both in close and lopsided elections (treatments pairs 1–3 and 2–4). Therefore we have substantively similar results between unweighted and weighted data in the turnout experiment.

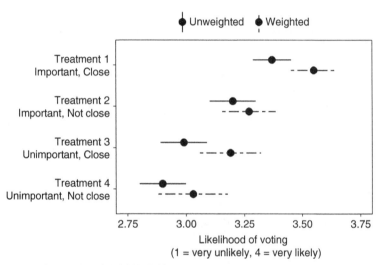

FIGURE 3.7 The average likelihood of voting across treatment conditions, unweighted and weighted data.
Note: Horizontal lines correspond to 95% confidence intervals. *Source:* Authors' survey.

The results of the abstention experiment with the weighted data are substantively similar to the originally reported results as well. Figure 3.8 reports the mean levels of negative emotions across the experimental groups using weighted data. Similar to what we observed in the analysis of unweighted data (reported in Figure 3.5), those in the *Important* election treatments reported feeling significantly more distressed, angry, upset, and guilty than respondents in the *Unimportant* election treatments. In addition, we find no evidence that these heightened negative emotions are driven mainly by extrinsic considerations in the weighted data (results not reported).

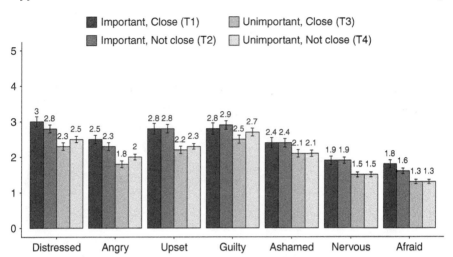

FIGURE 3.8 Negative affect emotions across experimental groups in the *Abstention* experiment, weighted data.

Note: Vertical lines correspond to 95% confidence intervals. *Source:* Authors' survey.

We obtain substantively similar findings to what we reported in the duty and group turnout experiments when we apply weights to our data. These results increase our confidence about the generalizability of our experimental results to the US adult population.

4

Theories of Protest Participation: A Review and a New Approach

Why do people join protests? What accounts for movements' dynamics? How do activists respond to, and anticipate, the strategies of the authorities and the reactions of the public? Sociologists, social psychologists, political scientists, and economists have all tackled these questions. Their theories are shaped by real-world movements – from the civil rights movement in the United States to new social movements in Western Europe, from democracy movements in the communist world to the Arab Spring. In this chapter, we briefly review this evolving scholarship, and extend our costly abstention theory to protest participation.[1]

Our review reveals some continuities between received theories of electoral and protest participation. The latter have shifted between stressing the inner motivations that lead people to protest, including their grievances and psychological responses, and the external incentives and resources that encourage participation. In both cases, rational choice theorists have shed light on the logic of protest but also failed to explain some dynamics, such as the fact that movements sometimes grow when the costs of participation rise. We learn much from theorists and empirical researchers about the impact of information and communicative stimuli; but they often fall short of explaining exactly why messages and information can be mobilizing. In this regard, the contributions of social psychologists have been especially fruitful.

In applying the costly abstention model of participation to protests, we echo the observations of prior scholarship. Many before us have observed that the objectives of protest organizers are a powerful mobilizing force – though, as with voting, this observation is not uncontroversial, since free-riding is thought to keep people who merely care about the outcome from taking part. Many

---

[1] See Oberschall (1978), Jenkins (1983), Walder (2009), Jasper (2011), Gupta (2017), and Kuran and Romero (2018) for reviews of the literature about social movements.

have remarked upon, and gathered valuable evidence about backlash movements, in which people go to the streets after the authorities repress earlier protesters, though few have noticed the anomalous aspect of this response from the standpoint of rationalist models. Many more have noted the apparent cascade dynamics of some protests and speculated about why people are drawn into the streets by the mere fact that many others are already there.

Rather than offering utterly novel observations, what we offer in this chapter and the next are two things. One is to stitch these "partial" effects into a single, consistent model. The second is to test the implications of the model with systematic evidence. This effort allows us to confirm that each parameter in our model has independently influenced people's decisions whether to protest, and, more importantly, to assess the relative power of each parameter in side-by-side comparisons.

GRIEVANCES AND RESOURCES AS PREREQUISITES FOR MOBILIZATION

A question that preoccupied theorists in the 1960s and 1970s was how people become sufficiently aggrieved that they join protests, and even rebel. Later, scholars decided that this was the wrong question. In most societies, there are many people who have acute social *grievances*; a sufficient supply of discontent is a constant. In addition, the aggrieved may prefer to free-ride on other people's activism. In the 1980s, a new generation of scholars identified organizational and financial *resources*, and *political opportunities*, as the sparks for contentious collective action, not grievances. Therefore, it was thought, the right question is: What kinds of resources might be deployed, and political opportunities taken advantage of, so that obstacles to collective action would be cleared? Later still, scholars refocused on the *identities* and psychology of protesters.

Ted Robert Gurr's *Why Men Rebel* (1970) exemplified the early, social-psychological orientation toward mobilization.[2] Gurr's central proposition was, basically, that when socioeconomic development produces a disjunction between people's expectations for advancement and their actual experience, they are prone to feel *relative deprivation*. The gap between the status they expect to achieve and their actual achievement leaves them disappointed, as does the gap between their achievements and those of others in their societies (see also Hirschman and Rothschild 1973). Disappointment fuels anger, and anger fuels rebellion.[3]

---

[2] See also Kornhauser (1959), Le Bon ([1895] 1960), Gusfield (1968, 1982), Geschwender (1968), and Smelser (1968).

[3] Huntington (1968) extends this logic to the development of political institutions, identifying a destabilizing gap between representative institutions when they run ahead of socioeconomic development.

In linking economic disappointment to anger and anger to mobilization, Gurr glossed over matters of organization, strategy, and the temptation to free-ride on the costly efforts of others. These shortcomings were noted by, among others, Tilly (1973, *inter alia*), and McCarthy and Zald (1973, 1977).[4] To these *resource mobilization* theorists, more important than grievances and discontent were the resources and opportunities available to protest leaders. Tilly (1973) found "aggregate psychological hypotheses" (like Gurr's) deficient. In his proposed alternative, the capacity to mobilize depended on "collective control over resources – land, labor, information, arms, money, and so on – which can be applied to influence the government"; demobilization means "losing collective control over resources" (p. 437). Along the same lines, McCarthy and Zald argued that movements need organizational and financial resources to sustain themselves. An example was the then-recent innovation of direct mailings as a technology that helped movement organizers reach would-be donors and participants.

Reacting against the absence of political context in resource mobilization theory, McAdam (1999) insisted that protests took off when a "political opportunity space" opened for them.[5] Movements, McAdam wrote, "are profoundly shaped by a wide range of environmental factors that condition both the objective possibilities for successful protest as well as the popular perception of insurgent prospects" (1999: 11). McAdam also deepened the critique of social-strain and psychological models. He decried their lack of "any discussion of the larger political context in which social insurgency occurs" (p. 11). He objected to the view, put forth or implied by some scholars, that movement participants are psychologically abnormal or socially marginal. He also lodged methodological complaints against social-psychological accounts. They infer the presumed psychological strain, such as relative deprivation, from objective conditions rather than from subjective data; they fail to document an over-time increase in relative deprivation as a precursor to movement activity; and they fail to compare the incidence of felt deprivation among participants and nonparticipants (1999: 13–19).

McAdam illustrated the importance of political opportunities in his study of the US civil rights movement. He pointed to several factors that created opportunities for black insurgency which had previously been closed.[6] McAdam emphasized that these structural and, in some regards, external shifts opened up room for black organizations and communities to mobilize for rights – they were the key actors in this story. But he also acknowledged the part played by

[4] See also Oberschall (1973), Wilson (1973), Schwartz (1976), and Orum (1972).
[5] Another key scholar of contentious politics who stressed resource mobilization, among other factors, is Sidney Tarrow (e.g., [1994] 2011).
[6] New opportunities were offered by the post-1930s decline of the cotton economy in the South and the great migration of blacks to northern cities, the emergence of black voters as a key force in certain northern states, participation of blacks as servicemen and women in World War II, and favorable governmental action in some domains.

"popular perception of insurgent prospects," allowing movements to attract large numbers of supporters. These ideas would be developed by later scholars who – as we shall show – would bring the tools of rational choice and of social psychology to the study of social movements.

Theories of social mobilization were always conditioned by real-world events. Developments in the 1980s in the United States and Europe brought attention back to the identities and ideologies of activists. They therefore represented a shift away from the sharp focus on resources and opportunities of the resource mobilization school. One real-world development driving this shift was the emergence of *new social movements*. Women's movements and movements of ethnic and sexual identity groups, environmental and antinuclear mobilizations; all were perceived as expressing "postmaterialist" values and objectives, and as superseding, or evolving alongside, the material concerns that had been the basis of mobilization in earlier decades (for example, the discussion in Jasper 2011: 14.4 and *passim*).[7] Ethnic conflict from Africa to the Balkans redoubled interest in identity-based mobilization (for instance, Pedersen 2002).

MOVEMENTS AGAINST AUTHORITARIAN REGIMES

If new social movements in Europe in the early and mid-1980s shifted scholars' focus, the antiauthoritarian and anticommunist mobilizations of that decade shook them profoundly. People took to the streets to protest highly repressive regimes in Southern Europe and the Southern Cone of Latin America. In 1989, awareness of the revolutionary power of social mobilization grew even stronger. The first unexpectedly large and open movement in a communist country that year was in China and was brutally repressed in Beijing's Tiananmen Square in June. In the fall of that year, movements erupted throughout the Eastern bloc and, in short order, in ethnic Soviet Republics.

To observers it was astonishing that throngs of demonstrators would go into the streets in such repressive places and that protests could escalate rapidly from small groups of ideologically committed dissidents to truly mass phenomena. Tens and sometimes hundreds of thousands of people, many of them previously uninvolved in dissent, came out into the streets and squares, at considerable personal risk. It was possible, *ex post facto*, to identify political openings that movement organizers were stepping into, such as Gorbachev's *glasnost* in the Soviet Union. But however one might "post-dict" these movements, what jumped out at the time was their *now-out-of-never* feel.[8]

The revolutions of 1989 through 1991 spurred a furious creativity among movement scholars. They wanted to explain why the movements had taken

---

[7] The US civil rights movement could be seen as a precursor to mobilization on racial rather than class lines, though economic justice was obviously of central concern to US civil rights leaders.

[8] This is the title of Timur Kuran's influential 1991 article, discussed next. He adopts the phrase from Vaclav Havel.

place at all and how they drew in so many ordinary citizens when the potential for state repression remained high (and, in Tiananmen Square, was put to use). The explanations were varied but tended to be more actor-centered than resource mobilization or political opportunity space had been. Early theoretical explanations of the revolutions of 1989 pointed to the moral tension that people experience between their (forced) public stance of support and their private unhappiness with the regime. Alternatively, scholars focused on citizens' exposure to new information about the regime and about the potential of civil society to resist it. An interest was rekindled in cascade models of collective action, which went back to Granovetter (1978): it seemed obvious, in 1989, that success bred success, with bystanders becoming more likely to join the more they saw others joining (though several explanations were offered for *why* people react this way.)

Two writers inspired by the 1989 Leipzig Monday protests capture these theoretical currents well. One is Timur Kuran, the other Susanne Lohmann. Kuran saw collective action as arising out of the moral tensions people face when they mask their true opinions of the communist regime.[9] He noted that people who dislike authoritarian regimes are forced to support them, or at least remain quiet, in public. But people naturally seek a kind of moral consistency between their public and private stances; tension between the two imposes disutility on them. They tolerate some tension between the two when the dangers and costs of self-expression are high. But the tension will become unbearably high if they observe many other people coming out into the streets and expressing their opposition. Every individual has a "revolutionary threshold," the number of others protesting publicly that will drive them to join the demonstrations. These thresholds exhibit tipping qualities: a small increase in the number of others protesting may tip large numbers of erstwhile bystanders to join them. The tipping dynamic explains the cascading of movements, when, suddenly, many bystanders' thresholds have been overcome and the movement surges.

Whereas moral tension moved individuals in Kuran's model, information moved them in Lohmann's. In normal times, government actions against the citizenry are dispersed and opaque to public opinion. Therefore, people are unsure whether the government is a "good" type or a "bad" type. When protesters take to the streets, their actions in effect aggregate this information and signal to others that the government is nefarious.[10] Hence, people who are targeted experience an intensified disdain for the regime, which encourages them to join protests: "the regime loses public support and collapses if the protest activities reveal it to be malign" (1994: 49).

---

[9] See especially Kuran (1991), but also his 1990 article and 1995 book.

[10] For other rational choice models in which government actions provide protesters a signal of government strength, see Przeworski (1991), Ginkel and Smith (1999), Pierskalla (2010), and Shadmehr and Boleslavsky (2015).

Lohmann's model rests on testable propositions. If she is right, bystanders join demonstrations after new information comes to light that leads them to update their beliefs about the regime's type; they come to see it as more nefarious than they had supposed. In other models, the information updating is about the protest's leadership: people learn that the protest leaders are good types or that success is likely (e.g., Shadmehr and Boleslavsky 2015, who were informed in part by the 2009 postelection mobilizations in Iran). These propositions, like Lohmann's, can be tested.

Like other rational choice theorists of protest, Lohmann was less troubled by collective-action problems than rational choice theorists of electoral turnout. Protest theorists resolve the collective-action problem by positing that hard-core activists derive utility from activism itself (e.g., Chong 1991; see also Wood 2003), a move akin to expressive theories of voting. Otherwise they posit that movements are carried out by organizations whose leaders offer their subordinates incentives to get them to participate (e.g., Lohmann 1994, Francisco 1995, de Mesquita 2010), a move akin to group theories of voting. McAdam (1999) questioned whether methodological individualism is an adequate approach to studying movements, given their deep social embeddedness. Participants are members of groups and networks, and these "insiders are threatened with the loss of member benefits for failure to take part" (McAdam 1999, p. xxxv). Yet if the benefits of taking part are selective incentives proffered by organizations, the participation of tens of thousands of common citizens with few organizational connections to the movements' leaders is not explained.

Theories inspired by the revolutions of 1989 were later enriched, and sometimes challenged, by empirical researchers. Another astute student of the Leipzig Monday protests was Karl-Dieter Opp (1991, 1994). Opp's research confirmed some of the theoretical assumptions and conclusions just discussed. Through extensive survey research he discerned a moral imperative that lay behind some individuals' decisions to join, echoing Kuran's theory. He wrote, "people often feel that they are obliged to participate when certain conditions are given, such as unjust political decisions of political bodies. Conformity to one's moral conceptions yields utility, whereas defection is costly" (1994: 103). But the impact of these moral and social pressures is unlikely to be linear. At high levels of repression, he explained, people feel justified in protecting themselves rather than acting on their sense of outrage; and people prefer that their friends and acquaintances take cover rather than expose themselves to physical harm when the risks are great (see also Klandermans 1984).

Some of Opp's evidence is in line with information-updating theories, though with more of a beauty-contest or emperor's-new-clothes dynamic than in Lohmann's story. State repression of protesters, he found, increases people's perception of the regime as vulnerable and the opposition strong: "repression leads citizens to believe that the support of government in the population will further decrease and the fading support must ultimately lead to reforms." He also offered a more psychological or behavioral interpretation of this effect: "In this situation a citizen will surmise that his or her personal influence will be high too" (1994: 105). Social pressures can play out in the same way. Opp contended that a person whose family members and friends are involved in protests will feel pressured to join in. More fully in tension with rational choice theories is the idea that the goals of collective action are themselves a source of motivation for protesters. He noted that the sought-after public good is itself a cause for protest.[11]

Similarly, rich empirical scholarship about the waves of mobilization in the Soviet Republics supported some early theorizing but also raised questions about several assumptions. Beissinger (2002) meticulously studied ethnonationalist movements in the Soviet Republics against the Moscow regime. He showed that, following the April 1991 massacre of protesters in Tbilisi, Georgia, the number of "backlash," repression-driven movements, and the size of these movements, outstripped nationalist and secessionist ones.[12] The power of repression to encourage mobilization is incompletely explained by information models, as we shall show in Chapter 6.

SOCIAL MOVEMENTS IN THE DIGITAL AGE

Social movement scholars have repeatedly, over time, been impressed by the power of new technology of the day to shape movement dynamics. Television, direct-mail techniques, fax machines, the Internet, and social media; each new technology has been used by activists and credited by scholars with shaping movement dynamics. Never has this been more true than in the digital age. Activists have made strategic use of video clips, cell phone images, and social media to spread information and mobilize support.

Indeed, the second decade of the new century has been a kind of golden age of mobilization. Many movements in this period were urban and youthful and (often) predominantly middle-class, their organizers making full use of the Internet and social media.[13] New-millennium protests displayed some of the edginess of the antiglobalization movements of the previous decade,

---

[11] See also related models by Przeworski (1991) and Blaydes and Lo (2012).

[12] He wrote that "backlash demonstrations against regime repression on average mobilized 43 percent more participants per demonstration than ethno-nationalist demonstrations in general and 60 percent more participants per demonstration than demonstrations in favor of secession from the USSR" (2002: 363). In a similar vein, in the context of explaining how movements become revolutions, Goldstone (1998: 130) wrote, "Where the government responds with unfocused repression that terrorizes a wide range of civilians and groups either unconnected or only loosely connected to the movement supporters, or where repression is inconsistent and arbitrary ... the movement is likely to attract supporters."

[13] Though, in authoritarian settings like China, governments also undertook countermeasures, by blocking or appropriating these same technologies. For an extensive insight into the Chinese regime's efforts to control and manipulate the Internet and social media content, see King, Pan, and Roberts (2013, 2014, 2017).

though the former were, on the whole, less violent (della Porta and Tarrow 2012, della Porta 2013). Even a partial list of major protest movements around the globe is long: postelection protests in Iran (2009); the *Indignados* in Spain (2011); Occupy Wall Street and its progeny in the United States (2011); Arab Spring protests beginning in Tunisia and spreading to Egypt, Bahrain, Yemen, Libya, and Syria (2011); "Chilean Winter" student protests (2011); the *YoSoy132* movement in Mexico (2012); massive protests in Ukraine (2003, 2004, 2013); in Brazil, protests against bus fare hikes (2013) and in favor or against the impeachment of the president (2015); Turkey's Gezi Park uprising (2013); Hong Kong's umbrella movement (2014); antigovernment protests in Venezuela (2014, 2017); mass movements in Hungary (2017); and the US anti-Trump resistance protests (2017).

It has not escaped observers' attention that the invention of the social media was followed by a spike in protest movements (Castells 2012, Bennett and Segerberg 2013). One function of digital technologies, whether in authoritarian countries, new democracies, or established ones, is to lower the costs of mobilization: organizers can now let hundreds or thousands of people know, instantaneously, that the protest will begin at, say, 6:00 P.M. on Saturday in the central square. Digital-age innovations can raise the costs of abstention by spreading pleas for solidarity or images of police crackdowns and abuses. Indeed, many young, urban, middle-class demonstrators have cell phones and many cell phones have cameras. So the streets are full of amateur photojournalists snapping pictures or recording videos of their fellow citizens being doused by water cannons or shot with rubber bullets. Just as images of police attacks on civil rights protesters in the US South were beamed through the nightly news into living rooms in the North, now images of police excesses captured on cell phone cameras are shared instantly.

A startling example of the power of digital technologies to mobilize Arab Spring protesters was when, in the days before the January 25, 2011 Tahrir Square demonstrations in Egypt, "several get-out-the-protest clips on YouTube strung together notorious scenes of police brutality captured by cell phone video cameras" (El-Ghobashy 2011, p. 7). Activists were not waiting for the police to attack their protests. Instead they used new media to remind people of past abuses, to get them out and into the Square.

Social movement theorists of distinct orientations might draw different conclusions about why YouTube videos of police abuse stir mass participation. Grievance theorists might view these as strategies to increase the level of discontent. Resource mobilization theorists might note that technological change in communications had placed greater resources in the hands of the opposition to an authoritarian regime. Rational choice theorists might infer that the Egyptian activists were signaling their strength to bystanders, thus causing them to update their estimate of the potential success of the movement.

A distinctive, though not entirely incompatible, interpretation comes out of social-psychological students of movements. Cognitive appraisal theorists, for instance, would focus on narratives of causation and blame that people impose on the police forces and authorities, and the emotional impact of these narratives (for a review, see Brader and Marcus 2013). We saw that new identity movements in the 1980s brought attention back to questions about how protesters understood their actions and those of their adversaries. But social-psychological work on movements has also attempted to systematize the role of emotions. These studies go well beyond simple ideas of "grievance," and they reject a strict dichotomy between rational and irrational or emotions-based actions. They distinguish *urges* (which are fleeting and tied to physical processes) from *moods* (which are more enduring and have no object) and from *moral emotions*, "feelings of approval and disapproval based on moral intuitions and principles, as well as the satisfactions we feel when we do the right (or the wrong) thing" (Jasper 2011: 143).[14] Though the language of psychologists is distinct, the ideas echo accounts of mobilization like Kuran's, where people strive for consistency between their public and private beliefs, or Opp's, where a drive to do the right thing, in one's own eyes or in the eyes of others, can lead people to mobilize even under the threat of repression.

With these developments and debates in mind, in the next section we redeploy our costly abstention theory of political participation, with some modifications, to gain traction on people's mobilization decisions. Our approach takes seriously the kinds of costs of participation, opportunities, and challenges of free-riding stressed in the resource mobilization and rational choice traditions, as well as the kinds of social, emotional, and moral factors that can drive up costs of abstention. Here and in Chapter 5, we hope to show that taking emotions seriously does not mean committing the methodological errors that McAdam – rightly – accused grievance theorists of making.

THE COSTLY ABSTENTION THEORY OF PROTEST PARTICIPATION

Why do people join public rallies, marches, demonstrations, and occupations in public spaces such as city streets or squares?[15] With some modifications, the theory of costly abstention from voting can help make sense of their choices.

Indeed, there is considerable overlap between the decision contexts of would-be voters and would-be protesters. As with voting, a key factor determining whether a person joins a protest is how much he or she cares about the

---

[14] For further orientations to recent social-psychological work on movements, see Van Zomeren et al. (2008), Van Stekelenburg and Klandermans (2013), and Jasper (2014). Pearlman (2013) gave an account of the emotional microfoundations of the Arab Spring protests.

[15] We have in mind protests that aim to get governments to alter their policies or actions, and sometimes press them to leave office. They may also target protesters on the other side of an issue (counterdemonstrations), or they may oppose other nongovernmental actors or events. We refer to nonviolent mobilization; armed movements take on distinct strategic dynamics; see, among others, Fearon and Laitin (2003), Kalyvas (2006), and Tezcür (2016).

aims of the movement. This is true even when the participation of any given individual is unlikely to make a difference to the protest's success. And it is true even though, in protests as in elections, the outcomes are usually public goods: everyone benefits (or suffers), whether or not they took part. As with voting, *both* participation *and* abstention impose costs. Sometimes the same event raises the costs of participation and abstention simultaneously, so that whether a person joins collective actions depends on the net effect. Though we use the language of "costs," emotional push and pull factors, involving emotions like anger, enthusiasm, and fear, are just as important as they can intensify or dampen the effects of the factors we consider.

To motivate our model, we consider some empirical regularities reported in the literature that a satisfactory model of protest participation needs to explain:

- The more a person cares about the outcome, the more likely he or she is to take part in protests (Klandermans 1984, Finkel, Muller, and Opp 1989, Opp 1994).
- The larger the number of people who take part, the larger the number of current bystanders who join in; and growth is sometimes rapid and accelerating, like a "cascade" (Klandermans 1984, Kuran 1991, Lohmann 1994, Siegel 2011).
- Repression of demonstrators sometimes suppresses protests, but sometimes it makes them grow, even exponentially (Opp 1994, Francisco 1995, Davenport 2007, Trejo 2014).

With these considerations in mind, we generalize our costly abstention theory to protest participation as follows. The factors influencing people's protest decisions include:

- their costs of abstention (A), which are intrinsic and psychological;
- their costs of participation (C);
- the value they place on the movement's goals – the net benefit they perceive in these goals being achieved versus the status quo or other outcomes (B);
- extrinsic social pressure and expectations of participation (D_E);
- the number of other individuals taking part, or expected to take part (N); and
- the level of repression inflicted on demonstrators (R).

These factors are related to the rewards from participating, P, through the following system of equations:

$$P = A - C + D_E \tag{4.1}$$

$$A = f(B[1 + N + R]), \quad f'(\cdot) > 0 \tag{4.2}$$

$$C = c + R^2/N. \tag{4.3}$$

Next we discuss these factors and the relationships among them. As most of them were already explained in the turnout model, we keep the discussions rather short except when introducing factors unique to the protest model.

Costs of abstention (A). People suffer dissonance when they share protesters' goals but do not take part, and this dissonance can induce them to act – abstention can be costly. For Kuran and, in part, for Opp, the dissonance arises from moral qualms. But the nature of the dissonance can be less cerebral. As with voters, would-be protesters' emotional responses can amplify or moderate their costs of abstention. Jasper (1998, 2014) suggested that moral and emotional impacts – "moral shocks" and a "morally grounded form of anger" – jointly spur protest. Other emotions besides anger, such as anxiety and enthusiasm, also influence the costs of abstention. We model costs of abstention as a function of differential utilities over outcomes, the size of protests, and the level of repression of demonstrators.

Differential utilities over outcomes (B). Citizens may care a lot or little about whether a protest's objectives are achieved. They may be hostile toward the protesters' objectives (and toward the protesters), in which case their value of B is zero. Alternatively, they may consider it a life-and-death matter that the protest succeeds, in which case their value of B will soar. We will offer evidence that people's willingness to protest rises and falls with how much they care about the outcome: if they don't agree with the protesters' goals, they will not take part. The exception would be the person who does not care about the outcome but faces strong extrinsic pressures (D_E) to take part. In our model, the causal chain connecting utility differentials over outcomes with a willingness to join protests is through the costs of abstention, which mount as B grows. This joint effect is modeled in equation [4.2].

This treatment of B implies that free-riding need not undermine protests. As noted, the goals of protests are classic public goods – jointly produced, nonrival, and nonexclusive in consumption – and participation is time-consuming and can be risky. Protesters are often, undoubtedly, driven by private side-benefits of participation, such as social approbation. But in our model, people may suffer straight-up disutility from not taking part, so their incentive to defect will be diminished. As with voters, when would-be protesters care a lot about the outcome, staying home may just not feel right.

In addition to its direct effect on people's willingness to participate, B also has an indirect effect through its relationship with two factors that we turn to next: the size of the protests (N), and the level of police repression (R). A person who eschews a movement's goals ($B = 0$) will not take part (absent sufficient extrinsic pressure), no matter how many others are in the street; and repression will not have a mobilizing effect on such individuals.

The strategic context – the size of demonstrations (N). When people decide whether to vote and whether to protest, the strategic environment comes into play, but in quite different ways. In many elections there is a clear percentage of votes cast that a candidate must cross if she is to win.[16] Therefore, the idea that a race can be close makes sense to voters. We argued earlier that close races raise the costs of abstention for would-be voters, though only when they see the outcome as both close and important.

The strategic context of protests is different for would-be participants. In general, the bigger the protest, the more likely it is to succeed. But there is no clear threshold for the number of participants who can tip the movement to success, and hence no meaningful sense of a movement being "close." If one-quarter of the three-quarters of a million or so demonstrators who jammed into central Kiev at the peak of the Euromaidan protests in the winter of 2013–14 had stayed home, would Viktor Yanukovych have remained in power?[17] If the Leipzig Monday protests in the autumn of 1989 had mobilized 40,000 people at their peak instead of 70,000, would the communist regime in the German Democratic Republic have persisted? Presumably, had the Monday protests never grown to more than 1,000-strong, the pressure on the Honeker government would have been much less. But where did the threshold lie between 1,000 and 70,000? The answer is: no one knows.

In our model, individuals who care about the protest's goals will bear higher costs of abstention, and thus will be more likely to participate, the larger the (expected or actual) size of the protests (equation [4.2]). This mobilizing effect of N parallels the effect of the closeness of election (γ) in the turnout model. Rather than focusing on the impact of their own participation in the protests, individuals who share the protesters' goals adopt the vantage point of the movement. This perspective urges them to take the same actions that many others take (or are anticipated to take) to bring about the desired outcome. Larger crowds might signal that "success" is imminent, and not participating in these circumstances would lead to greater psychic dissonance than when fewer people are participating. Still others might be drawn emotionally to protests when large crowds are involved; they might experience enthusiasm when they agree with their goals, driving up costs of abstention.

The size of protest also enters into the participation calculations of individuals through the costs of participation (equation [4.3]). Protest-related violence, often in the form of repression of participants by the police, can drive up costs of participation. The size of protest, however, can have a *decreasing* effect on costs of participation that are related to repression because of the safety-in-numbers principle: the larger the crowds, the lower the chances that a single individual will face a threat from the police or from counterdemonstrators (Kuran 1991, Lohmann 1994). Lower costs of participation are another channel for the mobilizing effect of N.

---

[16] Generally speaking, the percentage of the vote required to win, rather than the absolute number, is known ex ante; though in some electoral systems, the percentage cannot be known precisely.

[17] The "or so" here is quite relevant: estimates of the numbers of people who take part in protests are always guesses, often rough ones, and themselves part of the struggle between the authorities and the protesters.

Repression (R). Another key difference between elections and protests is the greater potential for violence in the latter. Elections are not violence-free, especially in developing countries. But the violent repression of demonstrators by the authorities is a fairly common feature of protests (Davenport 2007, Aytaç, Schiumerini, and Stokes 2017). It can run the gamut from mild efforts at crowd control to the police use of "less lethal" weaponry: water cannons, tear gas, batons, and rubber bullets. Their use can escalate, so that less lethal weapons are used in harmful ways or lethal weaponry (e.g., live bullets) can be deployed.

Though repression hikes the costs of participation, and could be considered a central component of these costs, we treat it separately in our formal model. We do so because it has the dual effect of driving up the costs of participation (equation [4.3]) *as well as the costs of abstention* (equation [4.2]). The reason why repression can increase costs of abstention is that bystanders who are sympathetic with the goals of protests or who feel affinity with them react with empathetic anger and moral outrage when they witness protesters suffering from police repression (Opp and Roehl 1990, della Porta 2013, Aytaç, Schiumerini, and Stokes 2018). These emotional responses lead to a psychic tension, or dissonance, increasing costs of abstention and encouraging bystanders to join the demonstrations. Modeling and studying repression separately will allow us to illustrate more clearly that costs of abstention are quite real.

Repression drives up costs of abstention only to the extent that a person shares the movement's goals. In equation [4.2], we depict this conditional effect by representing R and B as interacting factors. Some protests might have multiple or vague goals, in which case social identification with those who are already protesting could serve as a proxy for the value of B to potential protesters. Note that even in the absence of any repression or large number of protesters, some individuals will still bear the costs of abstention and thus are motivated to protest. These individuals are mobilized by a high value of B for whatever policy change is at stake.

In equation [4.3], we model the effect of repression on the costs of participation as nonlinear. They rise relatively slowly at lower levels but very quickly at high levels, when a person can realistically fear being jailed, injured, or even killed. Tiananmen protesters in Beijing in 1989 demonstrated astonishing courage but eventually fled, or tried to flee, when the tanks rolled in and the shooting with live bullets began. Gezi Park protesters in Turkey who had held out for two weeks finally fled in the face of very large deployments of police using highly aggressive methods, such as beatings. We focus here not on the overall level of repression but on *per capita* repression: its level relative to the number of people protesting. Hence the fraction R^2/N on the right-hand side of equation [4.3]. As mentioned, this formalization is consistent with the "safety-in-numbers" logic. It implies a cascade dynamic under some conditions, and therefore has some resemblance to the model in Kuran (1991).

An implication of our model is that repression can have ambiguous effects on the size of protests. For individuals who agree with the demands of protests,

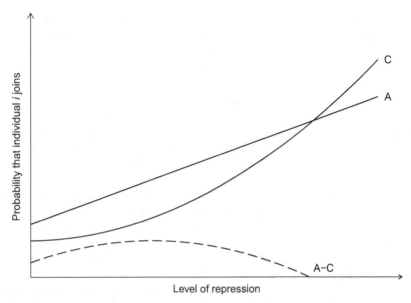

FIGURE 4.1 The impact of repression on the costs of abstention and participation.

at low-to-medium levels of repression, the costs of abstention in equation [4.2] might well dominate costs of participation. As repression increases, the costs of participation can mount more quickly than the costs of abstention, so that when repression is intense, it demobilizes people. This dynamic is illustrated in Figure 4.1, where the impact of the level of repression (horizontal axis) on the probability of a would-be demonstrator joining a protest (vertical axis) is shown. The line labeled *A* depicts the costs of abstention she experiences, which rise as a function of repression. The curve labeled *C* depicts the costs of participation, which also rise as a function of repression but in the nonlinear way suggested earlier. The inverted U-shaped curve marks the vertical difference between these two functions. Initially, as the level of repression rises, the person's probability of joining also rises, as the increase in costs of abstention outpace those of participation. But at higher levels of repression, this probability declines and the individual becomes more likely to remain (or return) home. The number of protesters at the initial stage, not considered in the figure, is also important as it affects the *per capita* effect of repression. The more people whom organizers can bring into the streets at the initial stages of the protests, the lower the threshold of participation for the potential protesters.

Costs of participation (*C*). Protest participation can be demanding in time, attention, and resources – more so, in general, than voting. Demonstrators may have to travel long distances and dedicate a big chunk of time to collective action. These costs in resources are indexed in our model with a lower case *c*. The asymmetry of costs is a major reason why protests typically involve a fraction of the number of people who turn out to vote, certainly of those who vote in national elections. The surveys we conducted in cities where major uprisings had occurred indicated that about 10 percent of the samples took part in the movements. Ten percent turnout in a national election would be abysmally low. The absence of a general civic norm in favor of protests, as opposed to norms in social networks and among subgroups and cultures, may also explain the relatively small size of protests.

Social pressure and expectations (D_E). As in the model of voting, we include a term, D_E, that indexes extrinsic pressures to take part. Whereas there is clearly a generalized social norm in most democracies that citizens should vote, there is no such civic norm about protesting. Indeed, democratic theorists have mixed feelings about protests.[18] Still, there are social expectations of participation among discrete groups in the polity. Opp (1994) offered evidence of the power of expectations among family, friends, and acquaintances in a person's social network to induce a person to turn out for a rally or demonstration. Chong listed the private benefits of protest participation that are disconnected from the movement's goals, including "the desire to gain or sustain friendships, maintain one's social standing, and avoid ridicule and ostracism" (Chong 1991: 9).[19] As in the voting model, we formalize the idea that norms can have an independent effect on a person's willingness to take part.

As implied by the stand-alone D_E in equation [4.1], an individual may comply with these expectations even when she does not feel particularly strongly about the outcome. But to the degree that norms of participation are internalized, these pressures fall under the rubric of costs of abstention. They are the equivalent of a conditional civic duty to vote, not in all elections, but in important ones.

SUMMARY

Taking into account the psychic and internalized costs that some people bear when they fail to take part in a protest allows us to make sense of their decisions to join. Social pressures and moral obligations also play an important part, as they do in people's decisions whether to vote. That staying home can impose costs on the abstainer explains why free-riding does not impede all participation in contentious collective action, even by people who are disconnected from organizations that can offer private inducements to encourage them to join in. Where would-be voters' and protesters' decisions depart most sharply is in the strategic context they face. The notion of being "close" to a threshold level required for success makes little sense for protesters, and they must often consider very substantial dangers and risks on the costs-of-participation side of the balance.

---

[18] For some recent criticisms, see Shapiro (2016) and Przeworski (2017).
[19] Chong also cites moral incentives to join the civil rights movement.

5

Testing the Costly Abstention Theory of Protest Participation

In this chapter we subject our costly abstention theory to empirical testing in the context of protest participation. We draw on our own original research as well as on a rich empirical literature on contentious politics. First, we offer evidence that agreement with the goals of the movement (B) is a powerful catalyst for participation. Next, we offer evidence, more suggestive than decisive, that people are especially prone to join protests when they both agree with their goals *and* perceive them as attracting many other people (N). Finally, we offer strong evidence of the mobilizing effect of police repression of demonstrators (R).

Our original research is from three recent movements: the Gezi uprising in Turkey in the summer of 2013, the *June of Fury* in Brazil (also in 2013), and the Euromaidan protests in Ukraine, which took place in the winter of 2013–14.[1] All three grew into national uprisings and became political crises with domestic and international consequences. The Gezi Park protests drew the world's attention to the Erdoğan government's growing authoritarianism. The Rousseff administration in Brazil never entirely regained its footing after the June 2013 protests. It faced more demonstrations during the 2014 FIFA World Cup matches and in 2015 over the impeachment process against President Rousseff. The Euromaidan protests drove the Yanukovych government from power, which in turn set off major conflicts between Ukraine, Russia, and Western governments.

Although many excellent, and highly relevant, studies of contentious politics exist, we undertook additional work in these three countries with an eye toward exploring the impact of factors identified in our theoretical model. Since observational data do not always lend themselves to isolating the impact of particular and discrete causes of people's actions, we were anxious to study additional instances of contentious politics with survey-experimental tools. In

---

[1] The research reported in this section was conducted in collaboration with Luis Schiumerini.

addition, social media opened up new opportunities for survey research of movements, sometimes in real time. In 2013, we became aware of an innovative research technique, spearheaded by David Samuels and Cesar Zucco Jr., who used the social media platform Facebook to recruit subjects into a survey experiment in Brazil (see Samuels and Zucco 2013, 2014). Lawrence (2017) also used Facebook to recruit Moroccans into a survey about the Arab Spring protests in that country. We followed their lead and, at the moment when the Euromaidan protests were at their height in Ukraine, we used Facebook to recruit protesters and nonprotesters into convenience samples that included experimental treatments, as the protests continued.

With the help of a network of researchers, we were also able to carry out traditional random-sample surveys of protesters and nonprotesters, with embedded experimental questions, in São Paulo and Istanbul. We and our assistants conducted interviews in all three locations. We interviewed protesters, activists, government and police officials and – in Istanbul and São Paulo – line officers assigned to the protests. Finally, we draw on convenience-sample surveys exclusively of protesters conducted during the height of protests in Istanbul, São Paulo, and Kiev, supplied to us by polling firms. We describe our data sources and techniques in greater detail in the next section.

Our choice of three research sites was also guided by our desire to explore the impact of repression on people's decisions to join or stay away from protests. The three cases selected all exhibited varying intensity of physical tactics against demonstrators – at first moderately high in all cases, and then reduced in Brazil and Ukraine, when the governments sought to defuse the crisis, and even higher than the initial level in Turkey, where the government chose to repress its way out of the crisis.[2] What's more, people's reactions to repression varied, in ways we will describe. Hence, to the degree that we are interested in an individual level of analysis, a background of varying but intense state repression of protesters allows us to study the impact of state tactics on individual citizens.

OVERVIEW OF THE PROTESTS IN THREE COUNTRIES

Gezi Park, Turkey. Turkey was rocked by protests from late May through mid-June, 2013. The movement's epicenter was Gezi Park, located next to Taksim Square in central Istanbul. The Erdoğan government had announced plans to turn the area into a shopping mall and mosque complex. In May, the Taksim Solidarity Committee established an encampment, to try to halt the development. At the end of May, municipal police attempted to dislodge the protesters, burning their tents and dousing them with water cannons, tear gas, and pepper spray. The movement soon spread. Within days, demonstrators were in

---

[2] We explain these varying responses in Aytaç, Schiumerini, and Stokes (2017). See Davenport (2007) for a review of the impact of regime type on repression of citizens.

the streets of Istanbul, Ankara, Izmir, and other cities, their numbers swelling to the hundreds of thousands. Memorable moments were early morning, June 1, when thousands of protesters from Kadıköy, on the Asian side of Istanbul, crossed the Bosphorus Bridge and made their way to Taksim to join the throngs already there; and June 8, when burly young men from football fan clubs, seasoned in resisting police crowd-control techniques, marched into the park.

On June 13, the police escalated to even more aggressive tactics in Taksim Square, this time succeeding in clearing the protesters from the square. On June 15, a vast police force attacked the park itself. Officers swung batons at the legs and upper bodies of protesters and blanketed the area with tear gas. This attack finally cleared the park and ended the protests. The authorities' harsh treatment of protesters – six were killed and hundreds injured – brought international condemnation of the Erdoğan government.

The June of Fury, Brazil. In June 2013, Brazil's Free Fare Movement (*Movimento Passe Livre*), an organization of graduate students from the University of São Paulo, held demonstrations against an announced public transport fare increase. A march held on June 6 was the first in a series of demonstrations against the fare hike. On June 13, the Minister of Public Safety of the State of São Paulo, Fernando Grella Vieira, authorized the deployment of shock troops to keep demonstrators away from the Avenida Paulista, a central artery of the city. The shock troops are a special unit of the state police. By the evening, video clips of police officers in riot gear aiming rubber bullets and tear-gas canisters directly at the demonstrators looped repeatedly on TV channels and the social media. Many civilians and several journalists were injured and arrested.

Rather than subsiding, as the authorities had hoped, the following week the number of protesters in São Paulo and other cities swelled to nearly a million and a half. At this point the civilian authorities began to sound a new note. The governor of the State of São Paulo, Geraldo Alckmin, announced that rubber bullets would no longer be used. At a press conference on June 16, Minister of Public Security Grella ruled out further deployment of shock troops. Soon after, the elected authorities made a key concession on bus fares. On June 18, less than a week after the crackdown, Mayor Haddad announced that transit fares would revert to their earlier level. The protests peaked two days later and then subsided.

Euromaidan, Ukraine. In 2010, Viktor Yanukovych became Ukraine's fourth president, five years after the Orange Revolution had forced a new election and kept him from acceding to the presidency. Yanukovych, and his Party of Regions, had strong ties to Russia.[3] But in 2012, dissatisfied with the terms Vladimir Putin was offering for Ukraine's entry into a Eurasian customs union, Yanukovych entered into talks about a possible Association Agreement with

---

[3] Yanukovych and his entourage had come up through the Soviet system in Eastern Ukraine; he had served in the early 1990s as governor of the Donetsk *oblast*.

TABLE 5.1 *Data sources in Turkey, Brazil, and Ukraine*

Location	Source	Sample	Date	N
Istanbul	Authors	Representative	Nov.–Dec. 2013	1,214
Istanbul	Konda	Convenience (protesters)	June 6–7, 2013	4,393
São Paulo	Authors	Representative	Dec. 2013	2,000
São Paulo	Datafolha	Convenience (protesters)	June 17, 2013	766
Kiev	Authors	Convenience (Facebook)	Dec.–Jan. 2013–14	602
Kiev	KIIS	Convenience (protesters)	Dec. 2013 and Feb. 2014	2,054

the European Union. This possibility was greeted with enthusiasm in Western Ukraine.

Yet negotiations with the EU were also difficult and on Friday, November 29, 2013, Yanukovych left an Eastern Partnership summit in Vilnius without signing an Association Agreement. Protests broke out in central Kiev that day. Early the next morning, on November 30, a special police force, the Berkut, brutally beat a small, lingering crowd in the Maidan. The reaction was swift. The following day, December 1, a Sunday, estimates of the size of the demonstrations on the Maidan ran as high as 800,000. Thus began a cycle of demonstrations that would help topple the Yanukovych government less than three months later.

To study common citizens' decisions to join these movements or stay away, we draw on a wide range of evidence, including the six surveys listed in Table 5.1.[4] Two of them are representative sample surveys that the authors conducted in Istanbul and São Paulo. They allow us to make comparisons between protesters and nonprotesters and to generalize our findings to the broader adult populations of the two cities. Our sample surveys in Istanbul and São Paulo included experimental questions, so they yield both observational and experimental data. In addition, we make use of important convenience-sample surveys exclusively of protesters. In Istanbul, on June 6–7, 2013, Konda Research and Consultancy interviewed protesters in Gezi Park. In São Paulo, on June 17, 2013, Datafolha interviewed protesters massed at the Largo de Batata plaza. The Kiev International Institute of Sociology (KIIS) carried out three waves of surveys of people demonstrating in Maidan Square, two of them in December 2013 and a third in February 2014. Each polling firm generously shared its original data with us. Finally, we used Facebook to recruit participants from among the adult population of Kiev into a survey which, again, included an experimental component. We carried out this survey in December 2013 and early January 2014, while the Euromaidan protests were ongoing.

---

[4] For more details, see Aytaç, Schiumerini, and Stokes (2017, 2018). See also the supplementary appendix for detailed information about the surveys.

Each kind of information and data that we make use of has limitations. Surveys conducted at demonstration sites allow us to be sure that respondents really did take part in the protests, rather than wishing, retrospectively, that they had. But these surveys don't allow comparisons between protesters and nonprotesters. What's more, subtle forms of bias may influence interviewers' selection of respondents in on-site convenience samples. In turn, even in random-sample surveys, when people report their reasons for joining protests (or for staying away), they may tailor their responses to fit an image that is appealing to them or (they believe) to the interviewer. Experimental designs can ameliorate these social desirability biases, for instance by making it harder for respondents to guess the goal of the study and adjust their answers accordingly (Steiner et al. 2016), as well as overcoming other obstacles to causal inference. But given the subject matter and our desire not to divorce the treatments too sharply from real-world phenomena, our experimental designs relied on respondents' hypothetical actions, raising questions about external validity. In the absence of any single ideal design or data type, our strategy has been to make use of a range of them. When they point toward similar answers, our confidence in our findings grows.

THE MOBILIZING EFFECT OF B

Intuition suggests that people who oppose a government's actions will be more likely than those who support them, or are indifferent, to join protests, and that protests are more likely to break out when governments pursue actions that are widely reviled. Yet we have reviewed two sources of skepticism of this view. Resource mobilization theorists note that the mere presence of an aggrieved public is not a sufficient condition for contentious politics. Rational choice theorists remind us that movement objectives are public goods and protesting is costly. Hence, there are solid theoretical arguments that B should not matter.

It is therefore important to assess how much people who protest are driven by policy goals or other kinds of movement objectives. One way that empirical researchers have done this is by demonstrating that people who protest care more about these goals than people who do not. Germans in the 1980s who were concerned about nuclear power, income inequality, environmental pollution, and a host of other issues were more likely than those who expressed less concern to say they had protested and that they would do so again (Finkel et al. 1989). Participants in the 2004 Orange Revolution in Ukraine evaluated the incumbent president, Leonid Kuchma, and the prime minister, Viktor Yanukovych, much more negatively than did nonprotesters (Beissinger 2013). Similar differences have been discerned between the mobilized and the unmobilized in protests against nuclear armament in the Netherlands in 1983 (Klandermans and Oegema 1987) and in the 1964 Mississippi Freedom Summer project in the United States (McAdam 1986).

TABLE 5.2 *Protesters' goals according to participants and nonparticipants, Istanbul*

In your opinion, how important are these goals for protest participants?	Participants (% very important)	Nonparticipants (% very important)	AKP voters (% very important)
Reversing development plans of Gezi park	76%	25%	7%
Opposition to government's conservative agenda	71%	29%	18%
Opposition parties/groups trying to weaken the government	27%	42%	54%
Making Turkey more democratic by getting people involved	72%	23%	6%
Showing reaction to police repression	71%	33%	23%
Protesting without a specific goal	20%	25%	31%

Source: Authors' survey.

In our survey of Istanbul residents, we asked respondents to assess the importance to the protesters of various goals, including halting the development of Gezi Park. In line with the movements' goals being mobilizing, three out of four self-declared protesters (about 10 percent of the entire sample) said that blocking the development of the park was indeed a crucial goal (Table 5.2). Not only did protesters share the goals of the protests to a degree that nonprotesters did not, the very interpretation of what these goals were, and what the protests signified, was sharply divergent, especially between supporters of Erdoğan's Justice and Development Party (*Adalet ve Kalkınma Partisi*, AKP) and opponents. Only one in four nonprotesters agreed that saving the park was indeed a very important goal of the protest, a number that drops to just one in seventeen among AKP supporters (Table 5.2).

Interpretations of what the protests meant and why people got involved fractured around a central and nearly all-encompassing cleavage in Turkey between seculars and devout conservatives. No such single divide exists in Brazil (Aytaç, Schiumerini, and Stokes 2017).[5] In our survey in São Paulo, about eight percent of respondents reported having taken part in the June protests. Seventy percent of these self-identified protesters cited the fight against corruption as a very important goal of the protest, and close to half cited reversing the increase in transportation fares and opposition to World Cup spending (Table 5.3). A smaller proportion of nonparticipants thought

---

[5] That was more true at the time of the protests than later in the decade, when corruption scandals and impeachment hardened the partisan divide between the supporters of the Workers' Party (*Partido dos Trabalhadores*, PT) and others.

TABLE 5.3 *Protesters' goals according to participants and nonparticipants, São Paulo*

In your opinion, how important are these goals for protest participants?	Participants (% very important)	Nonparticipants (% very important)
Reversing the increase in transportation fares	47%	38%
Opposition to government's spending for the World Cup	47%	31%
Opposition parties/groups trying to weaken the government	17%	13%
Fighting corruption in Brazil by getting people involved	69%	53%
Showing reaction to police repression	27%	19%
Protesting without a specific goal	9%	7%

Source: Authors' survey.

that these goals were very important, though the differences between the two groups are not as dramatic as in Turkey.

Another way to probe the importance of movement goals in mobilization is to ask those who are actually involved, and at the moment of mobilization, what their reasons were for joining the demonstrations. This research strategy overcomes the limitations in the German studies cited earlier and our own sample surveys just reported, where we expect measurement error when we ask representative samples about their participation. The advantage of on-site surveys is that we can be confident that actual participants are being tapped. The immediacy of events is also an advantage: when survey researchers ask respondents at the remove of weeks or months whether they took part and why, their memories may have dimmed. Of course, there are trade-offs: what we lose in on-site and real-time surveys is the ability to draw comparisons between participants and nonparticipants.[6]

In each of the cities of interest, survey organizations interviewed protesters on site, and provided us with their original, individual-level data. These should be considered convenience samples, though the polling firms went out of their way to try to avoid bias in recruiting respondents. In Istanbul, Konda, a private polling firm, carried out a large survey of protesters present in Taksim Square on June 6–7.[7] At that time the police had retreated from the Taksim area and the park served as a center of assembly for protesters and civil society organizations. The Konda researchers divided the park into 10 zones of equal

---

[6] Another potential drawback is bias in the selection of whom to interview among the protesters. See Miller et al. (1997) for a discussion of the nonquota, street-intercept survey method.

[7] See Konda (2013) for an overview of the results of this survey.

TABLE 5.4 *Protesters' motivations, Istanbul*

At what point did you decide to participate in the protests?	Protesters at Gezi Park
After seeing police violence	49%
When they began removing the trees	19%
Upon the statements of PM Erdoğan	14%
When the Taksim project was announced	10%
After seeing the atmosphere in Taksim	4%

Source: Konda survey – convenience sample of protesters.

size; they interviewed 4,393 demonstrators, in roughly equal numbers across these zones, in a nonstop shift over the two days. Among the questions they asked was, "what led you to join the protests?"

The modal response was not related to the goals of the protests but to police actions, a point we return to later (see Table 5.4). Two of the common reasons mentioned were the removal of Gezi Park's trees (19%) and the announcement of the Taksim development project (10%) These goals echoed those enunciated by protest leaders.

The mobilizing effect of *B* in São Paulo comes through clearly in on-site surveys, conducted by Datafolha. The firm interviewed 766 demonstrators who had assembled at the meeting point for the rally on June 17, the street *Largo de Batata*; Datafolha estimated the number of people massed there that day at 65,000. It asked demonstrators why they were there: 56% mentioned the bus-fare increase; 40% said they were protesting against corruption; and 31% mentioned police repression (Table 5.5). Hence the core demand of the *Movimento Passe Livre* was the modal reason demonstrators offered for why they had joined. The results are in line with those of a representative sample survey, conducted by Datafolha in July 2013, in which 77% of respondents cited opposition to the bus-fare increase as the key reason why people had taken to the streets.

Turning to Ukraine, an equivalent on-site survey was carried out in the Maidan by KIIS. They interviewed demonstrators in three waves. The first was on December 7 and 8, one week after the initial Berkut attack and the weekend of large demonstrations (N=1,037); the second on December 20 (N=515); and the third on February 3, 2014, less than a month before the Yanukovych government's demise (N=502). KIIS asked the protesters why they took part in the demonstrations, allowing them to offer several responses. As in Istanbul, the most frequent response was "because of repression of protesters." The second most common response cited the government's reluctance to enter the associate membership agreement with the European Union. Across the three

TABLE 5.5 *Reasons for joining the protests, São Paulo*

Reason	N	%
Protest against increase in bus fares	430	56
Against corruption	309	40
Protest against police repression	236	31
For better quality transportation	206	27
Against politicians	185	24
For free public transportation	107	14
For public security	102	13

Note: Respondents were allowed more than one response.
Source: Datafolha survey – convenience sample of protesters.

TABLE 5.6 *Reasons for joining the protests, Kiev*

Reason	N	%
Repression	1,361	66
Refusal of EU agreement	1,020	50
Desire to change way of life	968	47
Desire to change government	834	41
Dictatorship threat	383	19
Turn toward Russia	367	18
Revenge against government	156	8
Opposition leaders calls	116	6
Solidarity	127	6

Note: Respondents were allowed more than one response.
Source: KIIS surveys – convenience sample of protesters.

waves of the survey, half of the respondents offered EU associate membership as one of their reasons for getting involved (Table 5.6).

Both kinds of data reported so far – opinions gathered in representative sample surveys and from convenience samples collected at protest sites – have limitations. A key one is the leap involved from a person's statement that they share a movement's goals to the inference that these goals were truly a cause of their participation. Perhaps their opinions are simply correlates of a complex of traits and beliefs, which, together, are the real origins of the willingness to protest. In this case, what might look like a causal effect of *B* would in fact be an epiphenomenon of other factors. Even when an individual points to a movement goal as the reason they joined protests – keeping bus fares low, sparing a city park from development – they might actually have had less specific, perhaps less noble, reasons to take part. Recall Chong's list of private benefits from protests: "the desire to gain or sustain friendships, maintain one's social standing, and avoid ridicule and ostracism" (1991: 9).

To increase confidence in the causal effect of movements' goals on people's willingness to act, we devised survey experiments in each of the three epicenter cities of our cases – Istanbul, São Paulo, and Kiev.[8] The logic of the experiments was to randomly assign some respondents to a treatment that emphasized the movement's central goals and then ask them about their willingness to take part. We compared their willingness to that of a control group, in which respondents were simply asked the same outcome question – *How willing would you be to join protests if the movement flares up again?* – without any mention of protest organizers' goals. Reminded of the possibility of achieving its goals, the value of protest will appear higher to people in the treatment group. If the average willingness to join was higher among the *Goals* treatment group than in the control group, we would infer that B had a positive average effect on participation. Of course, what we are measuring is hypothetical, not actual, participation. But the hypothetical situation was in each case realistic and linked to an actual, recent protest.

For example, after the Gezi Park uprising in Turkey, the government quietly backed away from the park development project. We asked our *Goals* treatment group in Istanbul to imagine that the government was now again planning to develop the park, so that the value of the movement's goals (B) would now suddenly increase for those opposed to its development. In our São Paulo survey, we posited the hypothetical situation that the government reinstated the bus fare increase – which it had canceled during the protests – so, again, B would exogenously rise sharply for those who wanted the lower fares. In Kiev we asked respondents to imagine that the government had taken actions that further distanced Ukraine from the EU. In all cases, the outcome question was how likely the respondent would be to take part in protests if the movement flared up again, with answer options "very unlikely, unlikely, likely, very likely," coded from 1 to 4 in that order.

Indeed, though our findings vary from country to country, the common result is that *Goals* treatments had a mobilizing effect (See Tables 5.7, 5.8, and 5.9 in the appendix). In Istanbul, non-AKP voters were more willing to participate when posed with the hypothetical situation of the government reinitiating the development of Gezi Park. The mean willingness of non-AKP voters in the *Goals* treatment group was about 2.3 (on a 1–4 scale), compared to a mean of 2.0 of respondents in the control group. This statistically significant difference corresponds to a treatment effect size of about a quarter of a standard deviation of the outcome variable. We observe a similarly significant effect in São Paulo among those who held negative views of the national administration.

---

[8] The remaining shortcoming of our experimental design is that it measures, as an outcome, self-stated willingness to protest and not actual protest activity. It is unclear how a field experiment in protests might be carried off; we are unaware of any such studies.

In Kiev, the supposition that the government reasserted an anti-EU position had a mobilizing effect on our full sample, probably reflecting the fact that we recruited respondents on a social media platform that protest organizers had also used. All of these results suggest that, in the terms of our model, B is a trigger for a willingness to participate.

THE MOBILIZING EFFECT OF N

As a next exploration of our model, we consider the mobilizing effect of N, the number of other individuals taking part in protests. Our model posits two ways in which N matters. An expectation of large crowds increases the costs of abstention, though only among people who value the goals of the protests ($B > 0$). The second way is by decreasing the costs of participation: since there is safety in numbers, the risk of being the target of police or counterdemonstrators declines when the crowds are large. This latter effect is not dependent on B.

Many theorists and observers see a positive impact of movement size on bystanders' willingness to join, with explanations ranging from the viability of large protests to the safety in numbers they offer (see Klandermans 1984, Kuran 1991, Lohmann 1994, van Stekelenburg et al. 2010, Siegel 2011). But surprisingly little systematic evidence has been brought to bear on this question. Our own research suggests a magnetic effect of large crowds. In the same survey experiments that we deployed to gauge the impact of B, we also included a separate treatment which encouraged people to envision that a movement was underway and that it was large. We assigned a randomly selected subset of our respondents to a *Large Protests* treatment in which they read the following prompt: "Imagine that a month from now the government [undertakes an action contrary to the goals of the movement] and the movement flares up again. *You see or learn that a lot of people had gone into the streets, rallying together for change.* How likely would you be to participate?" The question thus combines the idea of large crowds with the *Goals* prompt.

In Istanbul, the *Large Protests* prompt significantly boosted opposition supporters' (i.e., non-AKP voters) willingness to protest, by about a quarter of a standard deviation above the control group (Table 5.7 in the appendix). This result provides experimental evidence for our theory's expectations: the size of the protests, N, entered into the equation for costs of abstention (A) through an interaction with B, the importance that individuals attach to the protest movement's goals. Yet the average willingness to protest of people in the *Large Crowds* treatment is only slightly larger than that of the *Goals* treatment, and the former is not significantly greater than the latter. When we focus on the young opposition supporters in our sample, the size-plus-goals effect begins to pull away from the goals effect alone. Young non-AKP voters in the *Large Crowds* group were about a third of a standard deviation more willing to protest than those in the *Goals* group, and about two-thirds of a standard deviation more willing than young non-AKP voters in the control group.

Turning to São Paulo, the average willingness to participate goes up when large crowds are implied, though the effects in the overall sample are small and statistically insignificant (Table 5.8 in the appendix). But we do observe a larger effect – again – among young respondents who are in opposition to the national government.[9] Once more, we see that N interacts with B, as our model predicts.

The amplification of N effects among the young, in Istanbul and São Paulo, is highly suggestive in the following way. Young people are frequently over-represented in protests. Konda (2014), for instance, report that about 51% of protesters in Gezi Park were between the ages of 21 and 30, compared to a rate of 22% in the Turkish population. This (negative) age effect has been a topic of discussion among scholars.[10] If we assume that the young are both especially gregarious and especially risk-tolerant (McAdam 1986, Wiltfang and McAdam 1991), their greater attraction to protests as N rises might help adjudicate between safety-in-numbers and social attraction/pressure explanations. Their greater tolerance for risk would lead us to expect them to be less sensitive than older bystanders to rises in N. That they appear to be more sensitive argues against the safety-in-numbers interpretation of the N effect. By default, our attention would then turn to a social-sensitivity explanation. The results can only be considered suggestive on this question; more research is needed to clarify the effects and the underlying social phenomena driving them.

Our Kiev Facebook survey departed in some ways from the other two. We included a separate *Large Protests* treatment, in which people were asked to "Imagine that in the near future a lot of people go out into the streets to demand changes together. How likely would you be to participate?" We also included a treatment that combined this prompt with *Goals*: "Imagine that in the near future the government undertakes actions that further distance Ukraine from the EU and a lot of people go out into the streets to demand changes together. How likely would you be to participate?" Here again, people seemed to be most stirred by the increase in B – the idea that the government had taken a step in the direction opposite from the movement's goals (Table 5.9 in the appendix). But there is also suggestive evidence of an N effect: the average willingness to protest of people in the combined treatment is the largest of the three (*Goals vs. Large Protests vs. Goals + Large Protests*), though not statistically larger than the average for the *Goals* treatment.

---

[9] High B – negative views of the government – are indexed here with evaluations of President Rousseff. The matter is complicated by Brazil's federal structure and the fact that opposing parties controlled national and state governments; for a discussion, see Aytaç et al. (2017).

[10] See, among others, Wiltfang and McAdam (1991), Dalton (2008), and Melo and Stockemer (2014).

THE MOBILIZING EFFECT OF R

"Maidan was waning every time when there were no [police] actions against it. When I was abducted by those guys, they tried to make me tell them the military secret – what to do with Maidan? I tell them, 'Listen, don't touch it at all, I'm telling you honestly, don't touch it, and it will go away.'"
– Yuriy Lutsenko, Ukrainian politician and Euromaidan activist.[11]

By telling antiprotest thugs who had abducted him that the government's best strategy would be to desist in repressing the Euromaidan demonstrators, Lutsenko is pointing toward the "punishment puzzle" (Davenport 2007). When a small group of protesters is subjected to police repression meant to end protests, sometimes bystanders join demonstrations, leading to even larger protests. Such instances have been identified by scholars in diverse contexts. Opp and Roehl (1990) studied nuclear power protests in West Germany in the 1980s; Opp (1994) focused on the Leipzig protests of 1989, Beissinger (2002) on nationalist movements in the waning period of the Soviet Union; Francisco (2004) reviewed massacres in the twentieth century; and Lawrence (2017) considered Morocco's Arab Spring protests. In all of these studies, repression was found to stimulate further mobilization. Our costly abstention theory captures this pattern of *backlash protests* by pointing to the mobilizing effect of the repression of demonstrators, R. Recall that in our theory repression has a mobilizing effect on bystanders only to the extent that they share the movement's goals or feel affinity with the protesters (high B). Repression drives up costs of participation *and* abstention; whether truncheons and pepper spray make protests grow or whither depends on the net effect. In this section we offer observational and experimental evidence for such mobilizing effect of repression in Turkey, Brazil, and Ukraine. In all three protest movements, police attacks on "early risers" did not merely precede but instigated the scale shift from protest to uprising.

As we saw earlier, survey respondents in Turkey, Brazil, and Ukraine offered police repression as a prominent reason for joining the protests (Tables 5.4, 5.5, and 5.6). In Turkey, a question in Konda's survey of protesters massed in Gezi Park was, "At what point did you decide to participate in the protests?" Nearly half of the respondents (49%) chose the answer, "after seeing police brutality." This was the modal response. In Brazil, "protest against police repression" was mentioned by 31% of protesters – the third most frequently mentioned reason. In Kiev, when the protesters were asked why they turned out, the most common response was "the brutal beating of demonstrators at the Maidan on the night of November 30; repression." This was the modal answer in each of the three waves of the survey, with 66% of respondents offering it as one of their responses.

Our fieldwork, which involved open-ended interviews of citizens, activists (like Lutsenko), and government and police officials in each of the three

[11] Lutsenko was interviewed on June 28, 2014, by Leonid Peisakhin and Anastasia Rosovskaya.

countries, also pointed to the mobilizing effect of repression.[12] Many people told us in interviews that they would not have become involved if not for police abuses of early protesters. One Gezi Park protester we interviewed in Istanbul had spent time during the protests practicing "social journalism," asking other protesters why they were there. Most people told her some version of the following: "When they saw the pictures or the video footage [of repression] they were scared. But they thought that they had to be there, because people like them were being attacked, persecuted, suppressed, and almost everybody said 'I had to be here.'"[13]

Another example comes from a conversation between a Turkish mother and daughter, relayed to us by the daughter in an interview. The conversation took place while they watched on television as the police let loose on demonstrators in Gezi Park in the first days of June, 2013. The daughter usually lived in Istanbul but was visiting her parents in the provincial city where they resided. On May 30, she learned on Facebook "that Gezi had exploded." She wanted to return right away "to join my friends who were out on the streets." But her mother, worried about her daughter's safety, pressured her not to go. "She threatened to disown me," the young woman joked, "so I had no choice but to stay." On Saturday, June 1, the mother and daughter were glued to the television – an opposition channel, since the mainstream, government-friendly media were avoiding the topic – watching coverage of events unfolding in Gezi.

We watched all day long, and finally my mom turned to me and said, "Ok go, please go and help your friends! These cops are a bunch of merciless, heartless men. Look how they are hitting all those unarmed young people. If they had any mercy they wouldn't do this to these innocent people." The next morning [Sunday, June 2], I left for Istanbul. Afterwards, when Gezi was occupied, my mom came to Istanbul and visited the park. She even baked some pastries at home to take to the kitchen in the park.[14]

When we probed the link between repression and mobilization, a frequent theme in our interviews was expressions of anger and moral outrage. An example comes from Kiev car enthusiast Dmytro Bulatov's account of why he founded the AutoMaidan, an organization that ferried people to and from the Euromaidan protests. Bulatov was spurred to action by the anger he felt, in December 2013, when he learned from a friend's Facebook post about efforts to get medical assistance for a young woman injured in the November 30 Berkut attack. He recalled in an interview (alluded to in our Introduction),

The police were attempting to take this girl toward a police vehicle, whereas [my friend] tried to rescue her from the police and take her toward an ambulance because she had been beaten and was covered in blood. Only then I turned on the television, opened

---

[12] See the appendix for details.
[13] Interview conducted by Gulay Turkmen and Susan Stokes, July 11, 2014.
[14] Interview by Susan Stokes in Istanbul, July 22, 2014. The mother is a supporter of the main opposition Republican People's Party (*Cumhuriyet Halk Partisi*, CHP).

the Internet, and, speaking honestly and plainly, I became enraged. You know, there are sometimes moments when you feel like you are coming apart because it is no longer possible to tolerate the situation. We phoned some friends to tell them that we have to put together a car protest.[15]

Bulatov's words convey the power of moral outrage and his experience of it as a nearly physical force ("you feel like you are coming apart.")

Our interviews in Brazil, too, suggested a link between repression, anger, and mobilization in the June 2013 protests. One activist told us, "when high repression takes place it awakens a feeling that all of us have the right to protest; so I think that it leads to an increase [in the number of protesters]. We observed this in June. There was much more anger."[16] These accounts are in line with our theoretical expectations – sympathetic bystanders who witness protesters being repressed experience empathetic anger and moral outrage. The resultant psychic tension ramps up costs of abstention, which in turn encourages them to participate in protests.

Of course, individuals do not always offer reliable reasons for their actions, and undoubtedly many people became aware of police abuses and were enraged by them but stayed away. Our theory predicts that repression should not have a mobilizing effect on everyone; only bystanders who share the movement's goals or feel affinity with demonstrators might react to police repression by joining the protests. Respondents in the on-site surveys conducted by Konda in Istanbul, Datafolha in São Paulo, and KIIS in Kiev were present at the mass rallies, and our qualitative evidence also draws on statements of protest participants and activists. This kind of evidence does not lend itself to comparing those who turned out with those who stayed home.

For these reasons, we return to the experiments reported on earlier. Recall that the experiment's treatment vignettes included hypothetical scenarios in which the movements were again stirring. One of these scenarios, the *Repression* treatment, highlighted police repression of protesters with the phrase "you see or learn that the police respond very aggressively to crowds that are protesting peacefully." The outcome question was respondent's self-assessed likelihood of joining the protests. We are interested in whether repression prompted more willingness to participate, in particular among the subgroups which our observational investigations indicated were sensitive to police attacks.

The results, with the average treatment effects reported in the appendix, indicate a mobilizing effect of repression. In Istanbul, the *Repression* treatment had a positive and statistically significant effect on the likelihood of protest mobilization among young individuals who were non-AKP voters: while the mean willingness of young non-AKP voters in the control group was about 1.8, on a 1–4 scale, it increased to 2.4 among their counterparts in the

[15] Leonid Peisakhin and Anastasia Rosovskaya interviewed Bulatov in Kiev on June 27, 2014.
[16] Interview conducted on May 26, 2014, in São Paulo by Luis Schiumerini and Susan Stokes.

Repression treatment group, an increase of about half a standard deviation in their willingness to protest. Similar effects are observed among young respondents who looked askance at the governments in São Paulo, and in the overall sample in Kiev.

These results are in line with the our theoretical proposition that repression will mobilize protesters, but are conditional on individuals sharing the movement's goals. They also echo the frequent finding that young people are prone to protest and may be less sensitive to its risks. As mentioned, Wiltfang and McAdam's (1991) concept of "biographical availability" of young people for risky protests implicitly attributed this pattern to their lower costs of participation. The young lack the kinds of "personal constraints that might increase the costs and risks of movement participation, such as full-time employment, marriage, and family responsibilities" (McAdam 1986: 70). It may also be that young people face higher costs of abstention – they may be more sensitive to social pressure and more emotionally reactive to what they view as morally unjustified attacks by the police.

SUMMARY

Our costly abstention theory of political participation, when applied to protests, yields important insights. In adapting the model to protesting, we modified it to take into account differences in norms surrounding electoral and protest participation and the distinct strategic environments of elections versus movements. What emerges from our own research into protest dynamics in three new democracies, as well as that of many others, is the centrality of protest goals as a core motivation for getting involved. Less robust but still suggestive is the power of numbers: people are more likely to join when they perceive that many others have joined or are likely to do so. In addition, our study underscores the ambiguities of state repression. It obviously drives up the costs of participation, but – perhaps less obviously – it also drives up the costs of abstention, at least for some people (government opponents, those who embrace the movements' policy goals, the young).

APPENDIX

Fieldwork and Surveys

Open-ended interviews. Interviews were carried out in São Paulo (May 2014), Kiev (May and June 2014), and Istanbul (July 2014). Open-ended interviews, usually lasting about two hours, were carried out with common citizens, activists, and police and government officials. A range of institutions and individuals were instrumental for identifying and contacting interviewees. In São Paulo, Fernando Limongi and Coronel Glauco Silva de Carvalho, Director of the Human Rights Directorate, São Paulo Military Police, helped us contact interviewees. In Kiev, the Institute for World Policy helped us to secure interviews. In Istanbul, Gulay Turkmen assisted us in securing interviews and served as co-interviewer and interpreter.

Konda's Istanbul convenience survey. Konda Research and Consultancy conducted a survey of protest participants in Gezi Park from the afternoon of Thursday, June 6 through the evening of Saturday, June 8, 2013, a time when the police had retreated from the area. As noted, the enumerators divided the park into 10 zones of equal size. They interviewed 4,393 demonstrators, in roughly equal numbers across the zones, in a nonstop shift over two days. In each zone, one interviewer conducted a maximum of 40 interviews in a two-hour interval. The goal of the survey was to provide a profile of the protesters. (For more details, see Konda 2013.)

Authors' Istanbul representative survey. The fieldwork for our Istanbul household survey was conducted by Infakto Research Workshop between November 20 and December 15, 2013. They interviewed 1,214 respondents. The sampling procedure of the survey was as follows. One hundred and one neighborhoods were randomly selected from the districts of Istanbul with a probability-proportional-to-size method. Streets in these neighborhoods, and then households on these streets, were chosen with a random selection table. In each household, the enumerator attempted to interview the household member whose first name began with the letter in the alphabet that came first. When the interview could not be completed with the selected respondent, the interviewer returned to that same household at a later time or date, to try to reach the selected individual. In the case of an unsuccessful second attempt, a new household was selected randomly. This process was repeated until an interview was secured. According to the research standards established by the American Association of Public Opinion, our response rate was 20.9 percent.

Authors' São Paulo representative survey. The fieldwork for the São Paulo survey was conducted by the firm *Análise, Pesquisa e Planejamento de Mercado* between November 20 and December 23, 2013. Interviews with 2,000 individuals, 18 years old and older, were conducted by phone. Households were selected using random-digit dialing, with quotas for neighborhood, gender, age, and level of education. In each household, the interviewer selected the household member by first name, as in the Istanbul author survey. In the case of an unsuccessful second attempt to reach this individual, a new household was selected randomly, and this process was repeated until an interview is completed. Our response rate was 10 percent.

Datafolha's São Paulo convenience survey. The survey firm Datafolha conducted a survey of protesters at the meeting point of Largo de Batata on June 17, 2013. This was the day that the protests ballooned as the news of police repression had broken, and the media and political elites started to criticize police actions. As mentioned, Datafolha estimated that 65,000 people participated in this protest. They interviewed 766 individuals at the main assembly point. To conduct the interviews the protest was divided in sectors, which corresponded to blocks. Each sector was assigned to an enumerator, who conducted separate rounds of interviews every hour in each block. Respondents were randomly selected. See *Contagem do Público da Manifestação Contra o Aumento do Transporte Público.*

Kiev International Institute of Sociology's convenience surveys. KIIS conducted surveys of protesters in Maidan Square. They did so in three waves, the first on December 7–8, 2013, one week after the initial Berkut attack, a weekend of large demonstrations (N=1,037); the second wave on December 20 (N=515); and the last one on February 3, 2014, less than a month before the Yanukovych government's demise (N=502). To select respondents, interviewers divided the Maidan into segments, which included public buildings occupied by protesters, and interviewed respondents in each segment.

Authors' Kiev convenience survey. Our Kiev survey was conducted between December 20, 2013 and January 19, 2014, when the Euromaidan protests were ongoing. We drew a convenience sample of 602 Facebook users who lived in Kiev and were at least 18 years of age. Following the lead of Samuels and Zucco (2014), we recruited respondents by placing ads in Facebook. People who responded to these ads were directed to Qualtrics. They were given the choice of taking the survey in Russian or Ukrainian.

SURVEY EXPERIMENT RESULTS

TABLE 5.7 *Istanbul: average treatment effects*

DV: Likelihood of participation	(1) Full sample	(2) Full sample	(3) Young participants
Goals	0.11	0.25*	0.41*
	(0.10)	(0.13)	(0.24)
Large protests	0.07	0.28**	0.74***
	(0.10)	(0.14)	(0.25)
Repression	−0.12	0.09	0.57**
	(0.09)	(0.14)	(0.26)

TABLE 5.7 *(Cont.)*

DV: Likelihood of participation	(1) Full sample	(2) Full sample	(3) Young participants
AKP voter		−0.87***	−0.44*
		(0.10)	(0.23)
Goals *AKP voter		−0.24	−0.61**
		(0.15)	(0.31)
Large protests *AKP voter		0.27*	−0.77**
		(0.16)	(0.34))
Repression *AKP voter		−0.18	−0.93***
		(0.15)	(0.30))
Constant	1.70***	2.02***	1.84***
	(0.07)	(0.09)	(0.17)
Observations	1,132	1,132	329

Note: Young participants are those below the age of 30. Ordinary least squares (OLS) regressions with robust standard errors in parentheses. *$p < 0.1$, **$p < 0.05$, ***$p < 0.01$. *Source:* Authors' survey.

TABLE 5.8 *São Paulo: average treatment effects*

DV: Likelihood of participation	(1) Full sample	(2) Full sample	(3) Young participants
Goals	−0.02	0.50**	0.73
	(0.08)	(0.24)	(0.49)
Large protests	0.03	0.22	0.92*
	(0.08)	(0.24)	(0.49)
Repression	0.04	0.43*	0.93*
	(0.08)	(0.24)	(0.52)
Support for government		0.09*	0.11
		(0.05)	(0.09)
Goals * support for gov.		−0.15**	−0.14
		(0.07)	(0.13)
Large protests * support for gov.		−0.06	−0.23*
		(0.07)	(0.14)
Repression * support for gov.		−0.12*	−0.18
		(.07)	(0.14)
Constant	1.96***	1.66***	1.95***
	(0.05)	(0.17)	(0.34)
Observations	1,927	1,927	502

Note: Young participants are those below the age of 30. OLS regressions with robust standard errors in parentheses. *$p < 0.1$, **$p < 0.05$, ***$p < 0.01$. *Source:* Authors' survey.

TABLE 5.9 *Kiev: average treatment effects*

DV: Likelihood of participation	(1) Full sample	(2) Young participants
Goals	0.36***	0.37
	(0.16)	(0.25)
Large protests	0.21	0.43*
	(0.16)	(0.26)
Repression	0.37**	0.45*
	(0.16)	(0.24)
Goals + large protests	0.41**	0.43*
	(0.16)	(0.24)
Goals + repression	0.57***	0.84***
	(0.16)	(0.23)
Constant	2.33***	2.18***
	(0.11)	(0.17)
Observations	624	250

Note: Young participants are those below the age of 30. OLS regressions with robust standard errors in parentheses. *$p < 0.1$, **$p < 0.05$, ***$p < 0.01$. *Source:* Authors' survey.

6

The Emotional Origins of Collective Action

Some emotions – psychologists call them *approach emotions* – drive people to act collectively. Most notable among them is anger. A flash of anger can stimulate a person to act; but particularly powerful in politics is moral outrage: the sense of having suffered an injustice, an injustice that would have been avoided if a political leader had acted differently. When people experience adversity that they see as *caused by* political actors, the sense of outrage and propensity to act collectively is all the stronger. In the terms of our model, anger and moral outrage can drive up the costs of abstention sharply.

In this chapter we consider two settings in which costs of abstention mount as a result of moral outrage. In both, explanations of political participation that rest on purely cognitive processes fall short. By bringing emotions into the explanation of collective action, we are able to tackle two puzzles. Why do people who lose their jobs often participate at lower rates – except when many other people are unemployed, in which case their rates of participation are not all that different than those of the employed? What is the link between repression and protest mobilization – demonstrated, but not fully explained, in Chapter 5?

To insist on the emotional dimensions of collective action is not to cast voters as unthinking citizens or protesters as angry mobs. As cognitive appraisal theory reminds us, much causal thinking and moral reasoning lie behind individuals' emotional responses. Nor does the focus on emotions drain the politics of collective action of all strategy. But strategizing is undertaken by elites – parties, campaigns, governments, activists – who either anticipate the public's emotional reactions, or fail to do so at their own peril.

UNEMPLOYMENT AND TURNOUT IN THE UNITED STATES

In 1982, Steven Rosenstone published an article in which he demonstrated that unemployed people in the United States vote at lower rates than do the employed.[1] He based this conclusion on a large survey conducted by the US Census Bureau and reported in the Current Population Survey (CPS), in which about ninety thousand Americans were asked about their employment status and about whether they had registered and voted in the November 1974 national election. Rosenstone offered two key findings regarding unemployment and turnout. The first was that unemployed people abstained at a higher rate than employed people. The second was that people who had been unemployed for a long period by the time before the November election were more likely to vote than those who had recently lost their jobs.

To explain both facts, Rosenstone invoked opportunity costs. "When the return from attending to an immediate, stressful personal problem, such as unemployment, is greater than the return from participating in politics," he wrote, "the opportunity costs of participation are higher. The higher the opportunity costs, the lower the possibility the citizen will participate in politics." To explain why the impact of unemployment on turnout dissipates over time, he reasoned that, once unemployment insurance is applied for and job searches are underway, "Adjustment to unemployment begins and its displacement of other concerns, such as politics, declines." (p. 36).

It is unsurprising that Rosenstone turned to varying opportunity costs to explain the patterns he observed. Prevailing theories of electoral turnout left him few alternatives. Early social-psychological models were ill-equipped to explain short-term variation in a person's willingness to vote, focused as they were on long processes of socialization. The most obvious moving part in rational choice models, in turn, was costs, including the bite that going to the polls would take out of a person's time budget.

But there are reasons to be skeptical of opportunity costs as fully explaining the dynamics that Rosenstone uncovered. For one thing, time-use surveys of Americans show that unemployed people have, if anything, too much time on their hands (Krueger and Mueller 2012). For another, the bounce-back effect – the increased willingness of the jobless, as their spells out of work lengthen, to go to the polls – turns out to be true in some, but not all elections. As demonstrated by Aytaç, Rau, and Stokes (2018), it is basically a feature of elections that take place during periods of recession – as the 1974 election had been. If one studies a long series of elections, from 1974 through 2012 – as we did, in each case with CPS surveys – it becomes clear that unemployed people's propensity to vote bounces back when labor conditions are bad but does not bounce back when labor conditions are good. That is, during recessions, the turnout rates of the longer-term unemployed converge with those of people who did not lose their jobs. But during nonrecession elections, turnout among the unemployed lags behind that of the employed, even if they have been unemployed for many weeks by the time of the election. Statistical analyses indicate that these differences do not reflect differences in the kinds of people who lose

---

[1] This section draws on collaborative work with Eli Rau.

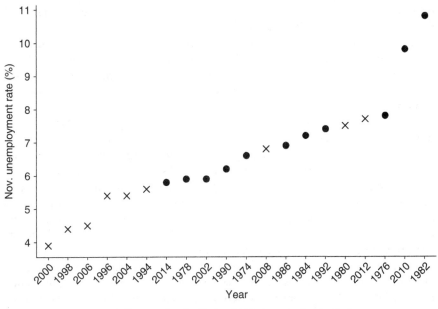

FIGURE 6.1 Bounce-back effect among the unemployed in the United States.
Note: "Bounce-back effect" indicates that the variable measuring the length of unemployment, *Weeks unemployed*, has a positive and significant (at the 5% level or lower, one-tailed) effect on turnout. Years are sorted along the x-axis by increasing rate of unemployment.
Source: Authors' analyses of the Current Population Surveys of the US Census Bureau and the US Bureau of Labor Statistics.

their jobs in recessions and in periods of expansion, or differences in the length of spells of unemployment in the two kinds of economies.

The pattern is shown in Figure 6.1, which plots the unemployment rates in November of each election year. The black dots represent years in which the unemployed became significantly more likely to vote as their spell of unemployment lengthened. The crosses mark years in which turnout remained low, even among those whose spell of joblessness was long, by the time of the election. With the exception of a few outliers, we can partition the years into two groups. All years with an unemployment rate greater than 5.7 percent exhibit the bounce-back effect; all years with unemployment below that rate exhibit no such effect.

There are three facts, then, that need to be accounted for: unemployed Americans vote at reduced rates; their reduced level of turnout persists when the job market is good; and their participation bounces back over time when the job market is bad. Rather than fluctuating opportunity costs, a better explanation takes into account the strategic incentives of candidates and the emotional responses of citizens. We offer that candidates – in particular, opposition candidates – politicize unemployment when it is high but ignore it when it is low. When opposition candidates pay attention to joblessness and blame it on the government, the unemployed become angry and their anger brings them back to the polls. When opposition candidates ignore joblessness, the unemployed are more likely to experience "withdrawal emotions" – guilt, depression, sadness – which social and political psychologists have demonstrated to be demobilizing (Carver 2004, Ojeda 2015).

The emotional impact of unemployment, like the impact of adverse events more generally, depends on how people attribute blame when bad things happen to them (Lazarus 1991). If they believe another agent is at fault, they are prone to become angry. Anger increases their sense of efficacy while at the same time dulling their sensitivity to risk (Lerner and Keltner 2001). If they think they or some disembodied force is at fault, they are prone to suffer shame and a sense of inefficacy (Brader and Marcus 2013). Emotional effects, then, cannot be read directly off an adverse event; they are shaped, instead, by the narratives of attribution constructed around them.

Reactions to unemployment depend on just such narratives. People's spontaneous reaction to job loss is, frequently, to feel depression and guilt. These are "withdrawal" emotions and discourage participation in collective action.[2] But the unemployed can be guided to see others as at fault, with important consequences for their emotional states and willingness to participate. When campaigns unfold in high-unemployment contexts, challengers point to the dire state of the economy and stress the government's responsibility for it (Vavreck 2009). In sum, in recession elections, the ingredients for the "bounce-back" are in place: challengers throw a spotlight on the bad economy and blame the government for joblessness, blame stokes anger, and anger encourages participation in collective action. The unemployed person who hears these messages of blame attribution shifts from depression to anger, and thus from emotions that demobilize to ones that mobilize.

Opposition presidential candidates in the United States do indeed spend more time in speeches talking about unemployment when the rate is high. An example is Bill Clinton. In his 1992 nomination acceptance speech, with the jobless rate at 7.5%, he uttered the word "jobs" 13 times, and "unemployment" twice. In 2000, with unemployment just at around 4%, the challenger, George W. Bush, did not utter either words even once in his acceptance speech. We analyzed nomination acceptance speeches of challenger candidates in presidential elections between 1976 and 2016. Figure 6.2 plots the November US unemployment rate in election years and the proportion of economy-related words in the nomination acceptance speeches of challenger presidential

---

[2] On emotional responses to job loss, see Linn, Sandifer, and Stein (1985), Feather and O'Brien (1986), Hamilton et al. (1993), and Price, Choi, and Vinokur (2002). On withdrawal emotions and the suppression of participation, see, among others, Carver (2004) and Ojeda (2015).

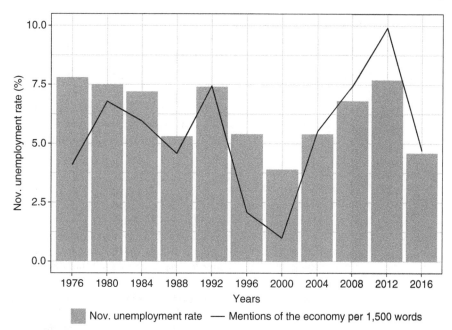

FIGURE 6.2 Unemployment rate and proportion of economy-related words in presidential challengers' nomination acceptance speeches in the United States, 1976–2016.
Note: We define incumbency by party, so in 1988, for example, Michael Dukakis was the challenger and George H. W. Bush the incumbent.

candidates.[3] The frequency of mentions of the state of the economy by challengers corresponds closely to the unemployment rate; the correlation coefficient between the two measures is 0.72.

Politicization and Anger Among the Unemployed: A Survey Experiment

So far we have seen that when US presidential campaigns unfold against the backdrop of high unemployment, opposition presidential candidates talk more about unemployment; and, in these contexts, the unemployed eventually vote at higher rates. But the strategic cultivation of anger among the unemployed by opposition candidates is not the only possible explanation for why they feel less downtrodden and more willing to vote when joblessness is widespread. It might be that the mere knowledge that many are out of work diminishes unemployed people's sense of guilt and self-blame, thus suppressing withdrawal emotions (see Incantalupo 2011).

To probe emotional reactions and adjudicate between this social and our favored political accounts, in October 2016 we conducted a survey experiment

[3] The source of the speeches is the American Presidency Project (www.presidency.ucsb.edu). The economy-related words selected for the analysis are jobs, unemployment/employment, growth, inflation, economy, and "out of work."

TABLE 6.1 *Experimental treatment vignettes in the* Unemployment *experiment*

Treatment	Vignette
Human Cost	Please read the following excerpt from a newspaper report about a woman who lost her job:
	"From May until November, Ms. Smith worked a seasonal job at the parks department. She spends her days sending out resumés that emphasize her bachelor's degree, which she received in January 2008, and her computer skills. 'I have to keep telling myself that I'm not a loser,' she said."
Blame	Please read the following excerpt from a newspaper report about a woman who lost her job:
	"From May until November, Ms. Smith worked a seasonal job at the parks department. She spends her days sending out resumés that emphasize her bachelor's degree, which she received in January 2008, and her computer skills. 'I have to keep telling myself that I'm not a loser,' she said."
	Some economists emphasize that there is a lot that the government can do to help create jobs and support firms that would like to hire workers. Rather than being a purely economic issue, unemployment is mainly a political issue – so if the level of unemployment is high and there are lots of people who lost their jobs, politicians and the government share much of the blame.

among unemployed Americans.[4] We exposed one treatment group to a framing meant to emphasize that others were suffering the harsh realities of being unemployed, implying that the respondent was not alone. This is the *Human Cost* treatment; it corresponds to the social explanation for the conditional bounce back. Subjects in this treatment were presented with a short news account of an unemployed woman struggling to find work (Table 6.1). Among the two-thirds of respondents who were assigned to read the *Human Cost* vignette, half were assigned to read an additional short text, on the following page of the survey instrument, that placed the blame for unemployment on politicians and the government. Hence this treatment added the kind of political rhetoric that, we argue, angers people and gets them back to the polls. We call this manipulation the *Blame* treatment. Finally, the *No Vignette* group only answered outcome questions, without reading any vignette.

We then asked posttreatment questions that allowed us to gauge respondents' emotional responses, elicited using the Positive and Negative

---

[4] The survey was conducted on October 19–22, 2016, less than one month before the presidential election. We surveyed an online sample of 750 unemployed American adults. Respondents were recruited through Survey Sampling International (www.surveysampling.com/). After dropping respondents who failed to pass an attention check filter, we were left with 706 respondents. For more details, see Aytaç, Rau, and Stokes (2018).

Affect Schedule (PANAS) scale that we also used in the experiments reported in Chapter 3. We asked about their willingness to vote in the upcoming November 2016 presidential election.

Box 6.1. The *Unemployment* experiment

Question. Why are the unemployed more willing to vote when joblessness is widespread?

Participants. 706 unemployed adult Americans recruited through the *Survey Sampling International* in October 2016.

Key finding 1. Participants are more likely to vote when they are exposed to political rhetoric that places the blame for unemployment on politicians and the government (*Blame* treatment).

Key finding 2. Participants in the *Blame* treatment report higher levels of anger than participants in the control condition.

Key finding 3. Reminding participants that others suffered during unemployment reduced their levels of guilt, but did not mobilize them to vote.

The impact of each vignette on the emotional states of respondents can be discerned by regressing self-assessed levels of anger and guilt on vignette assignment (Table 6.2). The *Blame* vignette significantly increased subjects' anger. The *Human Cost* vignette had no discernible effect on respondents' levels of anger, though it did significantly reduce their reported levels of guilt. So the emotional effects were as expected: a reminder that others suffered during unemployment reduced the withdrawal emotion of guilt, and a casting of blame on politicians nurtured the approach emotion of anger.[5]

The key point is that blame, uniquely, heightened respondents' willingness to vote. This willingness, as measured by the variable *Vote 2016*, was significantly higher among the people assigned to the *Blame* vignette (column 3 of Table 6.2); the *Human Cost* vignette produced no change in respondents' intentions to vote. The power of our *Blame* vignette to drive up intentions to

---

[5] The one unexpected result is that respondents who read the *Blame* vignette also reported a higher average level of guilt, though to a somewhat lesser degree than their increase in anger. Indeed, that treatment group evinced overall stronger negative emotions, while positive emotions were unaffected. We suspect that the heightened emotional state of respondents after reading the *Blame* vignette led them to be less precise in their use of the scale, selecting all negative emotions to express the extent to which they were upset. The PANAS scale is, in general, best at identifying overall positive and negative affect as opposed to precise emotions (Watson, Clark, and Tellegen 1988). Thus, while the PANAS scale does not enable us to fully isolate the specific emotion(s) driving the negative affect response of those treated with the *Blame* vignette, the behavioral outcomes of increased mobilization suggest that the response was indeed driven by the approach emotion of anger.

TABLE 6.2 *Average treatment effects in the* Unemployment *experiment*

	Anger	Guilt	Vote 2016	
	(1)	(2)	(3)	(4)
Human Cost	0.035	−0.259*	−0.152	−0.322
	(0.115)	(0.122)	(0.135)	(0.218)
Blame	0.422***	0.364**	0.264*	0.528**
	(0.117)	(0.124)	(0.137)	(0.218)
Vote 2012				1.179***
				(0.191)
Human Cost × Vote 2012				0.312
				(0.267)
Blame × Vote 2012				−0.479*
				(0.269)
Constant	2.247***	2.293***	3.770***	3.014***
	(0.081)	(0.086)	(0.096)	(0.157)
Observations	706	706	706	679

Dependent variable: spans columns (1)–(4); Vote 2016 spans columns (3)–(4).

Ordinary least squares (OLS) regressions with robust standard errors in parentheses. *$p < 0.05$, **$p < 0.01$, ***$p < 0.001$ (one-tailed). *Source:* Authors' survey.

vote is striking given the active mood of our sample when they came into the study. The 2016 presidential campaign had been riveting and emotional, and two-thirds of respondents in our *No Vignette* group said they were "certain" or "very likely" to vote in the upcoming election; 46 percent placed themselves in the "certain" category. Even though we might have expected our treatment to have limited effects because of a ceiling on likely turnout, the rhetoric of political blame still had a mobilizing effect.

This mobilizing effect emerges even more clearly when we focus on respondents who were less likely to vote. We had asked our respondents (before the vignettes) whether they had voted in the 2012 election. In the regressions reported in Table 6.2, we include Treatment × Covariate interactions to capture potential variation in the effects of our vignettes among respondents with different voting histories. Among those who abstained in 2012, the *Blame* vignette increased their intention to vote by about half a point on the five-point scale (column 4 in Table 6.2). The magnitude of this effect is highlighted by a comparison with the coefficient on *Vote 2012*: past voting history, one of the best predictors of future turnout, is associated with about a one-point increase on the five-point scale, only about twice the size of the *Blame* effect.

It is not surprising that people who voted in 2012 were not much affected by the *Blame* vignette. People who said they voted in 2012 expressed strong intentions to vote again in 2016, even in the absence of a mobilizing prompt. Seventy-nine percent of respondents in the *No Vignette* group who said they voted in 2012 indicated that they were "certain" or "very likely" to vote in 2016 (with 59 percent selecting "certain"). With a mean of 4.2 on our five-point scale, there was very little room to increase the voting intentions of these respondents.

Anger about the Economy and Verified Turnout
A drawback of the CPS data and of our experiment is that they only allow us to study people's self-reported willingness to vote, not actual voting. Because some abstainers are reluctant to admit that they failed to vote, self-reported turnout typically outpaces actual turnout (Holbrook and Krosnick 2010). To sidestep this difficulty we turned to the British Election Study (BES), which incorporates information from public election records about whether respondents went to the polls ("verified" turnout). We analyzed data from the 2010 BES, which, in the context of the Great Recession, also asked respondents about their mood vis-á-vis the economy. Unfortunately the BES 2010 did not ask about the employment status of respondents. Therefore what we study here is the impact of emotional reactions to the state of the economy on electoral participation among the general British population, not among the unemployed.

A question in the preelection wave of BES 2010 asked respondents to indicate the words that describe their "feelings about the country's general economic situation." The survey offered a variety of options, including *angry, happy, disgusted,* and *uneasy.* In the aftermath of the Great Recession, it is not surprising that many people said that they were uneasy (about 58% of the sample), disgusted (25%), and angry (23%) about the state of the British economy. BES respondents' moods were decidedly darker in 2010 than they had been in 2005, an election period when economic conditions had been better. A mere seven percent said they were angry about the economy in 2005.

The correlates of voting in the United Kingdom in 2010 will be familiar to students of turnout elsewhere in the world. Middle-aged and older people, those with higher incomes and more years of schooling, people who are married, and those who are union members; all are more likely to vote (see Model 1 in Table 6.3). So are people who expressed a stronger sense of a civic duty to vote. People who consider themselves as other than "White British" are less likely to do so.

Even with controls for widely recognized correlates of turnout, respondents who felt angry about the economy were more likely to go to the polls. Model 2 adds to the specification the binary variable *Angry (Economy)*, indicating those who expressed their ire on this dimension. The size of the effect of being angry on turnout is comparable to that of being married, about a six percentage point increase in the probability of voting.

An expectation is that among issues that people feel angry about, the ones they view as more important will have a greater potential to move them to

TABLE 6.3 *Being angry about the economy and turnout—BES 2010*

Dep. var.: verified turnout	(1)		(2)		(3)	
	Coefficient	SE	Coefficient	SE	Coefficient	SE
Female	0.12	(0.14)	0.14	(0.14)	0.12	(0.19)
Age	0.03***	(0.005)	0.03***	(0.005)	0.02***	(0.01)
Married	0.36**	(0.14)	0.34**	(0.14)	0.39*	(0.20)
Education	0.16***	(0.06)	0.16***	(0.06)	0.27***	(0.08)
Income	0.07***	(0.02)	0.07***	(0.02)	0.02	(0.03)
Union member	0.47**	(0.19)	0.48**	(0.19)	0.48*	(0.24)
Minority	−0.58**	(0.23)	−0.54**	(0.23)	−0.38	(0.35)
Civic duty	0.41***	(0.06)	0.42***	(0.06)	0.42***	(0.09)
Angry (Economy)			0.33**	(0.16)	0.57**	(0.24)
Constant	−3.28***	(0.38)	−3.39***	(0.39)	−3.18***	(0.55)
Observations	1,490		1,490		786	

Note: Models (1) and (2) consider the overall sample while (3) includes only those who consider the economy as the most important problem facing the country. Logistic regressions with standard errors in parentheses. $*p < 0.1$, $**p < 0.05$, $***p < 0.01$. *Source:* BES 2010.

the polls than the ones they view as less important. In BES 2010, respondents were asked to identify the "single most important issue facing the country at the present time," an open-ended question. Fifty-one percent (51%) of respondents considered the economy as the most important issue. When we limit the analysis to this set of respondents, anger boosts the likelihood they would vote by about ten percentage points (Table 6.3, Model 3). But people's anger about issues that were not very salient had little impact on behavior. Twenty-six percent (26%) of respondents reported feeling angry about immigration, 31% about the war in Afghanistan. But these were not high-salience issues: only 14% of respondents considered immigration the most important issue facing Britain; the corresponding number for the war in Afghanistan was 6%. Many Britons were angry about the economy *and* a majority of them judged it to be the most important issue facing the country.

Indeed, feeling angry about immigration (Table 6.4, Model 1) and about the war in Afghanistan (Model 2) do not have independent effects on one's likelihood of voting after controlling for traditional correlates of turnout. But if we limit the analysis to respondents who considered immigration or the war in Afghanistan as the most important issue (Model 3), the coefficient estimate for the effect of feeling angry about either of these issues on turnout is much higher and close to conventional levels of statistical significance (0.51, $p = 0.12$). A larger sample would probably result in a statistically significant effect, given the size of the estimate.

Since turnout reflected in these analyses is verified – those who said they voted are backed up in that claim with evidence from their polling places – we are reassured that expressed anger at the economy does indeed

TABLE 6.4 *Being angry about immigration or the war in Afghanistan and turnout—BES 2010*

Dep. var.: verified turnout	(1)		(2)		(3)	
	Coefficient	SE	Coefficient	SE	Coefficient	SE
Female	0.12	(0.14)	0.12	(0.14)	0.11	(0.31)
Age	0.03**	(0.005)	0.03**	(0.005)	0.03**	(0.01)
Married	0.36*	(0.14)	0.36*	(0.14)	0.37	(0.33)
Education	0.16**	(0.06)	0.16**	(0.06)	−0.08	(0.13)
Income	0.07**	(0.02)	0.07**	(0.02)	0.12*	(0.05)
Union member	0.47*	(0.19)	0.48*	(0.19)	0.69	(0.45)
Minority	−0.58*	(0.23)	−0.58*	(0.23)	0.37	(0.57)
Civic duty	0.41**	(0.06)	0.41**	(0.06)	0.45**	(0.14)
Angry (immigration)	−0.02	(0.16)				
Angry (war)			0.06	(0.15)		
Angry (either)					0.51	(0.32)
Constant	−3.04**	(0.41)	−3.08**	(0.40)	−3.85**	(0.92)
Observations	1,490		1,490		290	

Note: Models (1) and (2) consider the overall sample while (3) includes only those who consider immigration or the war in Afghanistan as the most important problem facing the country. Logistic regressions with standard errors in parentheses. $*p < 0.05$, $**p < 0.01$. *Source:* BES 2010.

predict participation. Thus the behavior of British voters in the shadow of the Great Recession strengthens the case for our theorized relationship between anger about the economy, a politically salient issue in the context of 2010 general elections in Britain, and turning out to vote. Britons who reported being angry about the economy during the 2010 general elections voted in greater numbers, even after accounting for an array of known correlates of turnout. The mobilizing effect of anger was most pronounced among those who saw the economy as the most pressing problem facing the country.

The mobilizing effect of emotions, and particularly that of anger, is illustrated in yet another context. As in Britain, there were general elections in Sweden in 2010; just like the BES, the Swedish National Election Study (SNES) verified the turnout of its respondents from public records. A question in the preelection wave of SNES asked respondents to what extent the election campaigns of either the Swedish Social Democratic Party or the Moderate Party, the two major parties in Sweden, made them feel angry. Respondents answered this question in a 0–10 scale, where zero corresponded to "not at all" and ten to "to a very great extent." Therefore the SNES 2010 presents us with another opportunity to test the relationship between anger and verified turnout.

Model (2) in Table 6.5 shows that those who reported higher levels of anger at political parties' election campaigns were more likely to vote, over and above the usual factors that drive people to vote, reported in Model (1). Even though the survey does not allow us to ascertain the reasons why people were made

TABLE 6.5 *Being angry about parties and turnout—SNES 2010*

Dep. var.: verified turnout	(1)		(2)	
	Coefficient	SE	Coefficient	SE
Female	0.43**	(0.20)	0.56*	(0.30)
Age	0.17***	(0.06)	0.24**	(0.09)
Married	0.91***	(0.24)	0.69**	(0.35)
Education	0.15***	(0.03)	0.24***	(0.05)
Income	0.24**	(0.09)	0.38***	(0.14)
Union member	−0.05	(0.21)	0.20	(0.31)
Foreign-born	−1.03***	(0.28)	−1.46***	(0.40)
Angry (campaign)			0.07**	(0.03)
Constant	0.02	(0.38)	−1.28**	(0.62)
Observations	2,019		1,304	

Logistic regressions with standard errors in parentheses. $*p < 0.1$, $**p < 0.05$, $***p < 0.01$. *Source:* Holmberg and Oscarsson (2017).

angry by the parties, we once again find an independent mobilizing effect of anger.

In sum, patterns of turnout and abstention among the unemployed are not well explained by models that leave out the emotional dimensions of voters' reactions. Rosenstone's signaling of higher opportunity costs, for instance, as the reason why the unemployed stayed away from the polls turns out to be insufficient. Indeed, though Rosenstone invoked opportunity costs, the language he used was redolent of emotional factors that went beyond a cost-benefit decision-making framework. He described job loss as a "stressful personal problem," and he quoted an unemployed person who talked about the effects of joblessness in terms of "beating yourself up" and a "loss of confidence" (p. 36). A more natural interpretation, and one supported by our research, is that job loss stirs withdrawal emotions – guilt, self-blame – and that these reactions are not fully reversed by the knowledge that many other people are in the same straits. To be fully reversed, joblessness needs to be framed as the fault of incumbent officeholders. Doing so stirs powerful approach emotions and brings unemployed voters back to the polls. In the terms of our model, anger and other approach emotions boost the costs of abstention. Our data focus on the unemployed, but undoubtedly the phenomena are broader. Strategic elite actors, in particular opposition candidates, understand that they can manipulate these kinds of emotions to their own benefit.

REPRESSION AND PROTEST IN TURKEY

In Chapter 5 we reviewed several explanations for backlash movements – why bystanders are sometimes mobilized by police repression of "early rising" protesters (McAdam 1995).[6] Some explanations revolve around the *information* that repression conveys to bystanders, information about the resolve and effectiveness of the government and of its opponents, or about the government's type ("good" or "bad").[7] In these accounts, repression conveys information that shifts people's factual beliefs in ways that encourage them to join the protests.

Quite a different perspective on backlash protests revolves around people's emotional responses to repression. Repression makes some people angry but also fearful. Up to some level of brutality, growing anger outweighs growing fear and brings them into the streets.[8] Our theory of costly abstention is closer to the social-psychological interpretations. People who are sympathetic with the goal of protest or who feel affinity with the protesters react with empathetic anger and moral outrage when they observe them being attacked by police. These emotional responses increase costs of abstention among bystanders, encouraging them to join demonstrations. Our model laid out in Chapter 4 captures this effect with the interaction of R and B on A.

We conducted a follow-up study in Istanbul to adjudicate between information- and emotions-centered explanations. The research strategy, as before, was to experimentally manipulate exposure to reminders of the Gezi Park violence and see whether these reminders make people more willing to engage in collective action. But the key question here is whether people who receive such reminders view the government as more vulnerable, dislike it more, or are more angry than those who do not. In statistical terms, we are interested in which (if any) posttreatment variables mediate the effect of the repression treatment on people's willingness to join collective actions.

Our Istanbul 2015 repression experiment takes advantage of the renewed salience of the Gezi Park conflict early that year. Though 18 months had elapsed between the protests and our experiment, in late 2014 news had broken that the Istanbul municipal government had set aside funds in its budget for the Gezi development project, spurring a public debate that was still ongoing in early 2015. In April and May, we interviewed an online sample of 833 adult Istanbul residents.[9] We randomly assigned respondents to a *Repression* treatment group, a *Placebo* group, and a *Control* group. Those in the repression treatment saw a collage of photographs that brought to mind the severity of police actions during the Gezi protests (Figure 6.3). The accompanying text read: "During the Gezi Park protests in 2013, many observers highlighted that

---

[6] The analysis in this section draws on collaborative research with Luis Schiumerini (see Aytaç et al. 2018).

[7] See among others, Przeworski (1991), Lohmann (1994), Opp (1994), Ginkel and Smith (1999), Pierskalla (2010), Blaydes and Lo (2012), Shadmehr and Boleslavsky (2015).

[8] See e.g., della Porta (2013), van Stekelenburg and Klandermans (2013), Jasper (2014), Lawrence (2017).

[9] Participants were recruited through benderimki.com, an online convenience panel. See the appendix for descriptive statistics of survey participants.

FIGURE 6.3 Istanbul 2015 survey: images used in the *Repression* treatment.

Box 6.2. The Istanbul 2015 *Repression* experiment

Question. Why does police repression mobilize bystanders to join protests?

Participants. Eight hundred and thirty-three (833) adult Istanbul residents recruited through an online panel in April–May 2015.

Key finding 1. Participants who were reminded of repression during the Gezi protests report greater willingness to participate in (renewed, future) protests. This mobilizing effect of repression is driven by people who oppose the government.

Key finding 2. Participants who were reminded of repression during the Gezi protests report higher levels of anger than participants in the control group.

Key finding 3. Formal mediation analysis identifies anger as the only effective mediator between being reminded of repression and being willing to protest; no mediation effects are observed for views on the ruling party.

the very harsh police action towards the protesters ended with at least six people being killed and several hundred badly injured."

Respondents assigned to the *Placebo* treatment group saw a postcard-like image of the Istanbul skyline at night with the statement, "This photograph was taken in Istanbul last month." The purpose of having a placebo condition was to rule out the possibility that any differences between the repression and the control group were due to the presence of images in the treatment groups rather than their content. People who were assigned to the *Control* group saw no image.

To probe differences in average willingness to join protests across the experimental groups, respondents were asked the following question:

> Recently it has been reported in the news that the Municipality of Istanbul allocated funds for the Gezi Park development in its 2015 budget. If the government and municipality decided to go ahead with the project, and the authorities began clearing the trees from the park and people started to go out and protest, how likely would you be to join the protests by going out and attending a rally?

They were then asked how likely they were to join the protests. Their responses were measured on a seven-point scale, ranging from *definitely would not* (coded one) to *definitely would* participate (coded seven).

Competing information- and emotions-centered explanations of backlash protests focus on distinct reactions that people have to police repression. It may change their views of the government or activists, or lead them to update their sense of which side is likely to prevail – or it may anger them. Of course, people might experience a mix of these reactions; but they are conceptually distinct and their presence or absence can be empirically probed. These distinct reactions can be thought of, in statistical terms, as mediators between repression and willingness to protest. To see whether reminders of repression shifted our Turkish sample's preferences, we surveyed, posttreatment, people's opinions of the ruling AKP party (Table 6.6). To see whether reminders of repression changed their beliefs about which side would prevail, we asked, posttreatment, about the government's strength and the likely success of future protests. A final mediator is the kinds of emotional responses that can increase the costs of abstention, in particular, anger. To see whether reminders of repression sparked emotional reactions, we again employ the PANAS scale. We instructed respondents in the *Repression* and *Placebo* treatment groups to think about the images they had just seen and to indicate the extent to which they felt anger, in addition to several other emotions. People in the control group were instructed to reflect on their emotions in the present moment. All respondents were asked to report their emotions on a five-point scale.

Results

The first result to note is that our Turkish respondents who were exposed to the repression treatment expressed greater willingness to join protests. This

TABLE 6.6 *Outcome questions in the Istanbul 2015 Repression experiment: potential mediators*

Explanations	Posttreatment questions
Information-oriented	If the government decides to go ahead with the project of developing Gezi Park, how effective do you think protests would be in stopping it? (*Protest Effective:* 1=Not effective at all; 4=Very effective) Do you agree or disagree with the following statements? (1=Strongly disagree; 5=Strongly agree) • The Gezi protests in 2013 were indicative of the AKP government's weakness (*Government Weak*) • The AKP government was confident of its handling of the protests (*Government Confident*) We would like to know what you think about each of the four political parties with seats in the parliaments. Please rate each party on a scale from 0 to 10, where 0 means you strongly dislike that party and 10 means that you strongly like that party. (*Views of AKP*)
Emotions-oriented	Below are a number of words that describe different feelings and emotions. Thinking about the images you have just seen, please indicate to what extent you feel each of the emotions below. (Control version: Please indicate to what extent you feel each emotion right now.) Angry, Outraged, Hopeless, Worried, Afraid, Hopeful (*Presented in randomized order; answer scale 1=very slightly or not at all; 5=very much*)

effect can be discerned in the first model in Table 6.7, a regression analysis of average treatment effects on the respondents' likelihood of joining protests, with the control group as the omitted category.[10] Were it not the case that the repression treatment encouraged mobilization, the interpretation of Gezi as a backlash movement or the verisimilitude of our experiment would be in question.

The second result to note is that the repression effect is driven by people who opposed the government: R interacts with B. Indeed, cognitive appraisal

---

[10] To deal with the problem of inattentive respondents, we inconspicuously recorded the time each one spent completing the outcome questions. We set aside about 12 percent of online respondents who spent less than five seconds – the minimum time required for thoughtful replies. There are no statistically significant differences in the number of discarded responses across the experimental groups. There is evidence suggesting that randomization was successful within this sample as well, as a likelihood ratio test from the multinomial logit regression of treatment assignment on participants' observable characteristics is statistically insignificant (Wald $\chi^2_{(28)} = 27.9$, $p < 0.47$).

TABLE 6.7 *Average treatment effects on willingness to protest*

DV: Likelihood of participation	(1a) Full sample	(1b) Full sample	(2a) CHP voters	(2b) CHP voters	(3a) AKP voters	(3b) AKP voters
Repression	0.38*	0.32*	0.62*	0.57*	0.17	0.20
	(0.22)	(0.19)	(0.35)	(0.33)	(0.23)	(0.23)
Placebo	0.01	−0.05	0.26	−0.01	−0.06	−0.13
	(0.21)	(0.19)	(0.36)	(0.36)	(0.18)	(0.19)
Intercept	3.23***	0.27	4.57***	3.17**	1.49***	1.21**
	(0.15)	(0.53)	(0.27)	(1.33)	(0.14)	(0.50)
Controls	No	Yes	No	Yes	No	Yes
Observations	694	641	217	204	173	161

Note: Controls include gender, age, education, interest in politics, and opinion about the country's direction. OLS regressions with robust standard errors in parentheses. $^*p < 0.1$, $^{**}p < 0.05$, $^{***}p < 0.01$. *Source:* Authors' survey.

theory predicts that not violence *per se*, but violence that is perceived as unjustified, provokes a backlash. In line with this prediction, the impact of repression in our samples was powerfully refracted through partisanship. The mobilizing effect of repression in the full sample is driven by its impact on supporters of the main opposition party, *Cumhuriyet Halk Partisi* (CHP) (Model 2).[11] AKP supporters who were assigned to the repression treatment were no more likely to say they would join the protests than were their copartisans in the control group (Model 3).

Having seen that reminders of repression can boost people's willingness to protest, especially people who oppose the ruling party, we turn to theoretically relevant mediators. Table 6.8 presents the effects of our treatments on these mediators among all respondents (top panel), CHP voters (middle panel), and AKP voters (bottom panel). The first result to notice is that people in the repression treatment were left angrier than people in the control group (column 1). This was true of CHP supporters. Recall that these CHP supporters in the repression treatment declared themselves more willing to protest than their copartisans in the control group (Table 6.7, Model 2). Hence, each of the links in the emotions-based explanation is present: *(1) repression produces anger, and (2) anger encourages collective action among opponents of the ruling party.* Of course, this evidence alone cannot be considered conclusive, but it is highly suggestive that emotions are the primary mediator between repression and protest.

[11] CHP and AKP supporters were people who said they would vote for the respective parties if there were an election next day.

TABLE 6.8 *Average treatment effects on potential mediators*

	(1) Anger	(2) Protests effective	(3) Government weak	(4) Government confident	(5) Views of AKP
			All respondents		
Repression	0.91***	0.03	0.21	−0.06	−0.69*
	(0.13)	(0.09)	(0.13)	(0.13)	(0.39)
Placebo	−0.84***	−0.05	0.14	0.11	−0.07
	(0.13)	(0.09)	(0.13)	(0.13)	(0.39)
Intercept	2.86***	2.84***	2.51***	2.83***	3.94***
	(0.10)	(0.06)	(0.09)	(0.09)	(0.28)
Observations	636	680	653	651	654
			CHP voters		
Repression	1.10***	0.10	0.13	−0.22	−0.29
	(0.19)	(0.15)	(0.22)	(0.22)	(0.24)
Placebo	−0.83***	0.26	0.12	0.22	−0.01
	(0.24)	(0.16)	(0.23)	(0.24)	(0.30)
Intercept	3.40***	3.03***	3.19***	2.32***	0.74***
	(0.17)	(0.11)	(0.17)	(0.16)	(0.21)
Observations	201	214	209	209	210
			AKP voters		
Repression	1.02***	−0.08	0.04	−0.01	−0.31
	(0.26)	(0.18)	(0.17)	(0.20)	(0.21)
Placebo	−0.78***	−0.34**	0.06	−0.06	−0.33
	(0.19)	(0.15)	(0.18)	(0.20)	(0.26)
Intercept	2.05***	2.56***	1.51***	3.92***	9.41***
	(0.16)	(0.11)	(0.11)	(0.13)	(0.13)
Observations	156	168	161	162	170

OLS regressions with robust standard errors in parantheses. $*p < 0.1$, $**p < 0.05$, $***p < 0.01$.
Source: Authors' survey.

Notice, however, that AKP supporters in the *Repression* treatment also became more angry than their copartisans in the control group, though they were no more likely to join the protests. Our interpretation is that AKP supporters were angered not by reminders of the authorities' harsh treatments of the protesters but simply by reminders of the Gezi protests. Indeed, AKP supporters overwhelmingly believed the government's framing, put forth during the protests, that the whole episode was a plot by foreigners against Turkey. A representative survey conducted by Konda Research (2014: 39–40) shortly after the protests asked whether protesters were "demanding for their rights and freedoms in a democratic manner" or were part of a "plot against Turkey."

Eighty-two percent (82%) of AKP supporters said it was a plot; only 10% of supporters of the the main opposition party (CHP) answered this way. Since most AKP supporters viewed the protesters as foreign agents or traitorous compatriots, their anger when reminded of Gezi protests is not surprising.

Did reminders of repression change people's beliefs about the likely success of the future protests? We asked our sample, "If the government decides to go ahead with the project of developing Gezi Park, how effective do you think protests would be in stopping it?" We also asked whether the protests had been indicative of the AKP government's weakness, and whether the AKP government was confident in its handling of the protests. *In no case did the repression treatment group's response pattern differ significantly from that of the control group* (see columns 2 through 4, Table 6.8). We therefore find little evidence from Turkey that repression mobilized people by changing their beliefs about the likely success of the movement.

Another explanation, implied by Lohmann's articles reviewed in Chapter 5, is that repression leads people to change the way they think about the government. In Lohmann's model, repression induces people to update their beliefs about whether the regime is a benevolent or malevolent type. Our experimental results weigh against these assumptions. In our overall Turkish sample, respondents in the repression treatment did exhibit more negative views of the government than those of respondents in the control group. But opinions of the government held by opposition CHP supporters in the repression treatment were no worse than those of their copartisans in the control group (see column 5, Table 6.8). Recall that CHP voters were the only subgroup whose willingness to protest was boosted by the repression treatment. Even if some AKP supporters were turned off by the government's heavy-handedness, both observational and experimental data indicate that these people were highly unlikely to protest. The insensitivity of CHP supporters' opinions of the ruling party to repression casts doubt on changing beliefs about the government's type as the link between police attacks and mobilization.[12]

One concern about our findings is that Turkish public opinion about the government might already have shifted during the protests in 2013, leaving little room for them to shift further in response to our experimental interventions. This is basically a question about the external validity of our experiment. Yet confidence that the results shed light on the 2013 backlash effect is boosted by the dynamics of public opinion and by election outcomes in Turkey, post-Gezi. To the chagrin of activists, Turkey remained basically the same politically polarized society before and after Gezi, with little growth in the number – large but not a majority – of government opponents. In our sample survey of Istanbul residents conducted about five months after Gezi, we asked how

---

[12] Table 6.8 shows that the effect of repression on views of AKP is larger in the full sample than among the AKP and CHP subsamples. The reason is that vote intentions are weakly correlated with assignment to the repression treatment and strong predictors of views of AKP.

respondents voted in the latest general election (2011), as well as their voting intentions in a future election. Ninety-three percent of respondents who voted for the AKP in 2011 stated that they would vote for the AKP again if an election were held that day.[13] National poll results point to the same conclusion.[14]

Our evidence thus far suggests that repression did not make opposition supporters dislike the government more or view it as more vulnerable. It simply angered them and their anger encouraged them to take part in collective action. To further investigate what mediates the effect of repression on mobilization, we employ formal mediation analysis.[15] Our goal is to identify the *average causal mediation effect* (ACME) – basically, what portion of the effect of repression on protest operates through mediating variables. We explore two potential mediators: emotions and opinions of the government – the only two that were influenced by the repression treatment (Table 6.8, top panel). Our measure of emotions, again, is the PANAS *anger* response; our measure of beliefs about the government's type is *Views of AKP*. Recent advances in mediation analysis allow us to study the simultaneous influence of two mediators on an outcome.[16] In the analysis we employ controls for potential confounders as recommended (Imai et al. 2011, p. 770), and use the observations not assigned to the repression treatment as the base category, following Imai and Yamamoto (2013).

Anger is the only effective mediator between repression and protest, in the full sample and among CHP supporters (Table 6.9). Consider mediation results just for those who support the CHP, 32 percent of our sample. In this model we assess mediation effects of anger and support for the AKP simultaneously. The corresponding ACME is 0.47. A result of this magnitude implies that the total effect of the repression treatment on CHP supporters' willingness to protest is almost exclusively channeled through anger (the mediated effect is 52% and the total effect is 61%). The analysis does not return significant mediation effects for views on the ruling party.

---

[13] This figure excludes people who are undecided or refuse to answer vote intention question. If we include them, about 83% of AKP voters in 2011 declared an intention to vote for AKP, which constituted about 52% of our sample.

[14] A national poll conducted by Konda Research in July 2013, right after the protests, revealed that about 52% of the Turkish voters reported an intention to vote for AKP if an election were held that day (Konda 2014). This figure is about the same as AKP's vote share in the latest general election before Gezi, 49.8%.

[15] The mediation analysis and discussion in this section is largely due to Luis Schiumerini and draws on Aytaç, Schiumerini, and Stokes (2018). On mediation analysis, see Baron and Kenny (1986), Bullock, Green, and Ha (2010), and Imai et al. (2011).

[16] See Imai and Yamamoto (2013). This method is appropriate when there is correlation among mediators. If the treatment influences the outcome through two correlated mediators, omitting one of them would be akin to introducing posttreatment bias, leading one to either overstate or understate how much the included mediator contributes to the outcome.

TABLE 6.9 *Mediation analysis of the impact of repression on protest participation*

Mediator	(1) Full sample	(2) AKP voters	(3) CHP voters
	Panel 1: single mediator analysis		
Anger	0.41***	0.11	0.37*
Views of AKP	−0.05	0.05	0.04
	Panel 2: two mediator analysis		
Anger	0.43***	0.13	0.52**
Views of AKP	0.06	0.05	0.02

Note: Numbers in cells are average causal mediation effects (ACME), estimated with the R package, *mediation*. In both single and two-mediator models, the treatment is repression, the other experimental groups are the base category, and covariates in the specifications are age, gender, level of education, interest in politics, and opinions about direction of the country. $*p < 0.1$, $**p < 0.05$, $***p < 0.01$. *Source:* Authors' survey.

Thus, our experiment suggests that the backlash movement in Turkey was fed by empathetic anger and not by repression-induced shifts in beliefs about the governing authorities or the opposition. Our qualitative evidence accords with this assessment. Field research, our own and that conducted by other scholars, found that many Turks already had firm views of the government and of protesters before the Gezi uprising. Among the bystanders who joined in, the anger and outrage they experienced in the wake of the late May 2013 police attacks were what pushed them into action (see especially Chen 2014). They expressed a sense of persistent and increasing irritation rather than a drastic shift in political perceptions or opinions. The metaphors they invoked were along the lines of the "drop in the bucket that makes the water spill over" rather than the "scales dropping from their eyes."

As an example, a young Turkish woman whom we interviewed had never taken part in protests before Gezi, though she had little sympathy for the ruling AKP or for then-prime minister Erdoğan. Her daily commute to and from work took her through the Taksim Square metro station. In early May, she had had several brief conversations with Taksim Solidarity members who were leafleting in the area. She recounted her outrage when, in late May, she saw images of Taksim Solidarity occupiers being doused with pepper spray and their tents being burned. She then joined the protests and spent most of the two weeks that they lasted occupying Gezi Park. Nearly all of the fellow demonstrators she spoke to mentioned the police violence as what brought them to the streets, describing it as one more irritant among many. "All these things built up, and then the park was the final drop for many people." The beatings in the park were "the last drop that made the glass spill over."[17]

[17] Interviewed by authors, Istanbul, July 17, 2014.

Political Elites and Emotional Responses to Repression
If costs of abstention mount when people experience anger and moral outrage, it is not surprising that protest leaders and government authorities strategize around mass emotional responses. They have done so in other contexts, such as the US Civil Rights Movement. Wasow (2016: 6) wrote that "While bigoted white civilians and police forces often responded brutally to these protests, the protesters themselves went to great lengths to avoid responding in kind. The logic was, in part, that occupying the moral high ground ... helped draw attention to and sympathy for the civil rights movement among persuadable members of the more moderate white majority."

In places like Montgomery and Selma, Alabama, the activists' and authorities' first-best outcome was to provoke violence on the other side, thus casting the others as the violence-prone aggressors, while retaining an image of nonviolence on their own side. Some police and local elected officials were adept at keeping their officers in line, but others – such as Selma's Sheriff Jim Clark – let their emotions get the best of them and found themselves and their departments on the defensive (Chong 1991: 26–7). Acts of official violence were no news to activists and African-American communities in the South, but they were more surprising to observers outside of the region, and some of these outsiders were mobilized after learning of abuses by sheriffs' departments and local authorities. The same was true of some participants in the Freedom Summer campaign (McAdam 1986).

More recently, Euromaidan activists and Ukrainian officials attempted to control their own side, at least from visible acts of violence, and to goad the other side into committing such acts. The original Berkut attack had taken place in the dead of night, presumably to keep it out of the public eye (although, with cell phone cameras everywhere and the press not far away, it soon became public). Later, on December 11, 2013, with activists having erected barricades and sustaining a constant presence in the square, the Berkut was sent back into the Maidan. Their orders from the Minister of Interior Affairs were to clear barricades but refrain from physical contact with demonstrators (Walker 2013). Yet the protest organizers did not miss the opportunity presented by the Berkut's return to the square and publicized images of a phalanx of officers in riot gear. According to Tatiana Chernovol, a protest leader and harsh critic of the government, the protest movement at this point "exaggerated ... they said people were being killed. No one was killed, some people were beaten, but [in general] the police acted very peacefully at that moment."[18]

For their part, governments that use harsh measures against demonstrators often try to craft a counternarrative that justifies their actions. During the Gezi protests in Turkey, Prime Minister Erdoğan called the protesters "looters" in

---

[18] Interviewed by Leonid Peisakhin and Anastasia Rosovskaya, Kiev, June 25, 2014.

the early days of the protests.[19] As the protests continued unabated, Erdoğan's rhetoric escalated, to the point – as mentioned – that he characterized the movement as a foreign plot against Turkey.[20] In sum, in settings in which emotional responses lie behind bystanders' reactions to state violence, the authorities and movement leaders strategize around the backlash. They aim as much at shaping citizens' emotional responses as at influencing their beliefs or preferences.

SUMMARY

In this chapter we underscored the importance of emotional factors in explaining collective action, factors that typically lie outside the lexicon of economic theories for political behavior. First, we explored the emotional impact of unemployment on turnout. We showed that the economic context and elite rhetoric jointly shape people's emotional responses to joblessness, and that these emotional responses in turn encourage or discourage political participation. Next, we considered protest mobilization, focusing on instances in which police repression of protesters brings erstwhile bystanders into the streets, rather than scaring them away. We found little evidence that heavy-handed police actions made people revise their beliefs about the balance of force between government and protesters, nor did it seem to jolt them from indifference toward the government to seeing it as malign. Instead, in Istanbul, anger was the link between repression and mobilization.

The common theme in these studies was the power of emotional costs and dissonances to bring people into the polling places and onto the streets. Our analyses demonstrate the advantages of taking emotions seriously in explaining citizen participation. Rather than downplaying strategic action, we suggest a marriage of strategic action by campaigns, ruling parties, and activists, and emotional reactions among the mass public.

---

[19] *Radikal* newspaper, June 2, 2013. The word he used was *çapulcu* which can also be translated as marauders or bums.
[20] See e.g., *Radikal* newspaper, June 3, 20, 22, 2013.

APPENDIX

TABLE 6.10 *Istanbul 2015* Repression *experiment: respondent characteristics*

Variable	Repression	Placebo	Control	Overall
Observations	277	278	278	833
Male	0.40	0.43	0.50	0.44
Age	31.22	30.68	29.83	30.57
Education	3.11	3.21	3.03	3.12
Employed	0.49	0.53	0.47	0.49
Partisan	0.62	0.62	0.58	0.60
Participant in Gezi	0.27	0.24	0.23	0.25
NGO member	0.22	0.17	0.19	0.19
Interest in politics	1.88	1.75	1.85	1.83
Opinion of country's direction	2.77	2.75	2.74	2.75
AKP voter	0.24	0.26	0.28	0.26
CHP voter	0.34	0.31	0.27	0.31
Importance of Gezi park	2.83	2.77	2.74	2.78
Past turnout	0.88	0.91	0.89	0.89
View of protesters	2.58	2.57	2.52	2.56

Note: Education refers to the highest level of education completed, measured on a scale of 1–4 (1=primary; 4=college degree). *Employed* is a binary variable indicating individuals who report being full-time employed. *Partisan* is a binary variable indicating individuals who report feeling close to a political party. *Participant in Gezi* is a binary variable indicating individuals who report having participated in Gezi protests. *NGO member* is a binary variable indicating individuals who report being member of a nongovernmental organization (NGO). *Interest in politics* is a 1–4 scale of level of interest in politics where 1 is very interested and 4 is not at all interested. *Opinion of country's direction* is a 1–4 scale of opinion about direction of the country, where 1 is very good direction and 4 is very bad direction. *AKP voter* and *CHP voter* are binary variables indicating individuals who report a vote intention for AKP and CHP, respectively. *Importance of Gezi park* is a subjective evaluation of the importance of preserving Gezi park, where 1 corresponds to "not important at all" and 4 to "very important." *Past turnout* is a binary variable indicating individuals who report having voted in the last general or local elections. *View of protesters* is a 1–5 scale of view of Gezi protesters where 1 is very negative and 5 is very positive.

The Istanbul 2015 *Repression* Experiment

Table 6.10 reports the number of observations and the averages of several demographic and other characteristics for each experimental group.[21] The similarity of these observable characteristics across the groups suggests that random assignment was successful. Additionally, a likelihood ratio test from the multinomial logit regression of treatment assignment on these

[21] There was an additional arm in our experiment (not reported) that explored the mobilizing effect of solidarity as part of our broader project. Together with this treatment the number of respondents reaches 1,111.

characteristics is statistically insignificant (Wald $\chi^2_{(28)} = 22.64$, $p < 0.75$). This test is also insignificant if applied to the data set that excludes respondents who do not pass attention checks (Wald $\chi^2_{(28)} = 27.89$, $p < 0.47$), or to the data set that excludes both these respondents and those who fail to respond to the willingness to protest question (Wald $\chi^2_{(28)} = 28.70$, $p < 0.43$).

7

Conclusions: Criticisms, Extensions, and Democratic Theory

We promised at the beginning of this book a theory of political participation that would rest on sensible assumptions and explain real-world behaviors. A chief task of this final chapter is to outline how we have made good on this promise. Another is to anticipate areas of skepticism about our theory and respond to them. We take on these tasks in the first part of the chapter. Later we reflect on the broader implications of our study by addressing two questions. The first has to do with electoral behavior. Does the theory of costly abstention, which we developed to help explain turnout, change the way we think about voters' choices in candidate elections, once they show up at the polls? The second question shifts to the terrain of democratic theory. Does our rethinking of why people take part in elections and protests change our assessment of these two instruments of popular participation?

THE EXPLANATORY POWER OF COSTLY ABSTENTION

Prominent theories of participation in elections and protests offer many insights but also display serious shortcomings. What follows is a reminder of several of the key innovations of our theory and the facts it helps explain.

Overcoming free-riding. Our model explains why people take part in collective action even when it is costly to do so and when they will reap the benefits of public good provision whether or not they participated. In short, it explains participation in collective action to produce public goods. Rational choice theorists modeled voting as a special case of the collective action problem. In voting, the small part an individual contributes to the production of a collective good actually falls to zero, in expectation that casting the tie-breaking vote is vanishingly unlikely.

The free-rider problem becomes tractable in our model because people pay individual psychic costs when they abstain. Understanding that costs are two-sided, and must be borne both by participants and by abstainers, helps explain how people side-step the free-rider problem. When abstention is burdensome, "free-riding" is no longer free.

Another related anomaly is the supposed disconnect between a person's willingness to take part and how much she cares about the outcome of collective action (the B term). We theorize that costs of abstention are a positive function of the importance of outcomes – the more important the outcome seems to a person, the more willing she will be to vote or protest. What's more, we document this causal effect with hard data. Thus we bring theory into line with basic intuition and with observable facts about the world. For their part, theorists of social movements have long acknowledged and documented that people who care more about, say, a nuclear plant not being built or a government falling are more likely to join protests on these issues. But they have not incorporated this fact into a theoretical framework that also lays out the disincentives people have to protest.[1]

The strategic settings. That people bear costs when they fail to participate also helps make sense of the common observation that individuals' willingness to participate is sensitive to the actions of others. When would-be voters see their fellow citizens splitting pretty evenly between a candidate they favor and one they oppose, they may be more willing to add their vote to what they hope is the winning side. We posit that costs of abstention rise as a function of the closeness of the race (γ), though only to the extent that the outcome of the race matters to them ($B > 0$). As the race tightens, they are more emotionally roused; to the extent that they see the situation through the eyes of their candidate, their sense of urgency grows. A similar dynamic is found in protests. As the number of people already on the streets swells, adopting the movement's vantage point and seeing "victory" within reach makes those who value the movement's goals to suffer costs of abstention and be more willing to participate in protests. In addition, costs of participation may decline as the protesters may anticipate being shielded from the police by large crowds.

Explaining why rising costs of participation can be followed by higher rates of participation. One fact that remains unexplained by existing theories is that people frequently respond to higher costs of participation by turning out *more*. Empirical researchers have strong intuitions about situations of this kind – for instance, when restrictions on ballot access fail to depress turnout to the degree expected (Valentino and Neuner 2016). Their intuition is that groups targeted by these restrictions can also be mobilized by the effort to exclude them. Empirical students of movements, likewise, have strong intuitions about the mobilizing effect of actions that raise the costs of protesting. For instance, della Porta (2013: 153) wrote that a "sense of injustice, as well as the creation

---

[1] In our review in Chapter 4, we mention works by authors such as Finkel, Muller, and Opp (1989), and by Chong (1991), that most approximate this kind of model, though with formalizations quite different from ours.

of intense feelings of identification and solidarity, prompted by repression can increase the motivation to participate."

Our theory lays out explicitly the logic behind these intuitions. It does so by broadening the lens beyond the costs a person bears when she takes part, to encompass the ones she bears when she abstains. The battle for participation is between the resources people need to expend if they go to the polls or to the streets, and the psychic dissonance and social pressure they might endure if they do not. The battle can be quite private and internalized, not requiring that other actors monitor would-be voters and demonstrators, and hold them to account for their choices.

A single event or action can drive up both kinds of costs. Laws that restrict ballot access make it harder for the targeted groups to vote, but also make it harder for them to stomach staying away from the polls, and easier for leaders in their communities to mobilize their anger. Police attacks on protesters can also stir moral outrage, pushing people to act. What explains their willingness to join in is not the ebbs and flows in the costs of participation, but the balance between these costs and the costs of abstention.

Emotions and participation. Much theorizing about collective action has been psychologically naïve. The human mind processes information, forms perceptions, recognizes group attachments, engages in moral reasoning, and experiences emotions. People perceive candidates and their proposals not just as good or bad for them, but also as good or bad against standards of morality, values, and tastes. They react emotionally to candidates' images, affect, and statements, and these emotional reactions can freeze their evaluation of politicians, even when the latter modify their positions or tone (Conover and Feldman 1984). Likewise, as we have seen, moral outrage and anger can trigger protest.

Emotional appeals by political actors and activists heighten people's costs of abstention. If a candidate manages to make a would-be participant angry and to blame his opponent for the state of the world that is the source of her anger, the costs of abstention rise. When they rise, so do the would-be voters' likelihood of making it to the polls.[2] If police actions (and activists' framing of those actions) elicit anger and moral outrage among like-minded bystanders, they become more willing to go into the streets.

It is especially important to come to grips with the emotional dimensions of participation decisions at a time when populist politicians are ever more in evidence. These politicians employ antiestablishment appeals and whip up support with an *us-versus-them* discourse, claiming that "the power elite are unable or unwilling to represent ordinary citizens" (Barr 2009: 31). They

---

[2] Though other emotions, such as fear and euphoria, also influence participation decisions, they have not been the focus of our study. Brader (2006), for instance, focused on the effects of campaign ads that feature appeals to fear and enthusiasm. See Brader and Marcus (2013) for a general review of scholarly findings on emotions in politics.

prefer direct, vertical ties with their followers, sidestepping party organizations, and are dismissive of institutions of horizontal accountability. They stoke anger and resentment among their followers, blaming the establishment and institutions for the grievances of the ordinary citizen. Our study sheds light on the mobilizing power of populists, though it also suggests that emotional appeals and reactions are a normal part of democracy. Populism is distinctive in the degree to which leaders lean on the emotions of constituents, rather than by the fact that they do so.

ADDRESSING SKEPTICS

In this section we outline possible objections to our theory and respond to them. The discussion takes the form of a series of questions that skeptics might pose and our answers. Some of the skepticism is connected to how much social-scientific ink has already been spilled in models of participation. Reflecting on the reception of their minimax model, Ferejohn and Fiorina lamented in 1975 that "nearly everyone has his own theory of how voters behave," and "most of these theories do not agree with the one presented in our article" (1975: 920). Forty years later, we expect a *there's-nothing-new-under-the-sun* reaction, and try to forestall it in what follows.

- Rational choice models already anticipate a cost of abstention in that citizens feel a duty to vote (D). Ignoring this duty presumably would impose dissonance on the abstainer. How is the theory of costly abstention different?

There are key differences. We broaden the set of drives that can lead people to vote, which include anxiety, anger, or enthusiasm about outcomes. What's more, whereas rational choice theorists sever duty as a stimulus to vote from the importance people see in the outcome of the election, in the costly abstention model, the two are causally connected. In fact, people's internalized conviction that citizens have a duty to vote rises and falls with their sense of the importance of an election, as we have shown. So the construct of duty as it appears in rational choice models should be reconceived as one component of the costs of abstention.

- A conditional duty to vote in important elections sounds like rule-utilitarian theory.

It does. But there are important differences between rule-utilitarian and costly abstention models. Rule utilitarianism features ethical voters who don't think egocentrically about the costs of voting. Instead they look at costs, like everything else, from the vantage point of a social planner or their preferred party. They stay away from the polls when voting is costly, not because they can't be bothered but because they have a (conditional) duty to abstain. The presumed duty to abstain derives from a social planner's imperative to minimize the social cost of voting, and hence of turnout. In our theory, citizens abstain when they don't want to bear the costs of voting, which they consider in an ego-centered way, and when these costs outweigh any costs of abstention that they might also experience. Our would-be participant is a more recognizable human being, subject to self-centered calculations of costs while still being potentially moved by a sense of duty, social pressure, or psychic friction from abstaining.

- Aren't costs of abstention a lot like the anticipated regret that drives people to the polls in the minimax model?

They are in some ways similar. But our model goes beyond the kind of radical uncertainty over outcomes that defines the mindset of the minimax decision-maker; we posit that there are social-psychological and emotional bases to participation decisions. Our model, what's more, does not rest on the controversial assumption that people anticipate a tied election, and we add to the evidence already available that relatively few people vote because they anticipate a tie.

- Social movement theorists are not as flummoxed as voting theorists by free-riding. In addition, many of them have studied social network influences on protest participation, as well as the moral-emotional underpinnings of collective action. What does your theory add?

Some rational choice theorists of movements take free-riding very seriously and are at pains to explain why it does not block all collective action (e.g., Chong 1991). Other rationalist models of protest wave away free-riding by positing that participants are members of organizations, the leadership of which can offer selective incentives for them to act. But this resolution of the free-rider problem rings less and less true in the age of digital mobilization. Others note the private benefits from protesting and moral imperatives to do so. But – as with theorists of voting – they tend to downplay any connection between protest participation and people's adherence to movements' goals. Highly sophisticated studies that take the social psychology and emotional substrate of action into account tend to study these factors one by one, rather than placing them in a full explanatory model.

We also have been surprised by how little hard data lies behind common claims of movement theorists, for instance – as noted in Chapter 5 – about the dynamics of movement cascades, or about repression as a stimulus to act. Our data-gathering efforts have allowed us to go deeply into the underlying reasons that lie behind backlashes and cascades. We have been able to assess the *relative* importance of the factors derived from parameters in our model. Hence we come away with a sense that the impact of B is large and robust, whereas that of N, though discernible, is less powerful.

- Why study voting and protesting together?

These are two essential tools that common people can use to engage in the public life of democracies. (Citizens in authoritarian systems also engage in protests, and sometimes exercise their voice in elections, though under strong constraints.) Our book emphasizes the large areas of overlap, and smaller disjunctions, in people's decisions to take part in each. Participation in both is driven by the balance between the burdens of taking part and those of staying away; both would-be voters and would-be protesters are subject to moral tensions as well as social pressures; the overriding factor in both cases is how much a person sees as at stake in the outcome; and emotions like anger play a large part in propelling people to act. What is needed is not a theory of participation in elections and another theory of participation in protests, but a single theory which, with some modifications, makes sense of both. We hope to have contributed to building such a theory.

Scholars of elections and protests can learn from each other to think in fresh ways about their subjects. A case in point is voter ID laws. Empirical researchers documented the failure of these laws to suppress turnout to the degree expected, and speculated that media coverage framed these laws in ways that "make some voters very angry," and that this anger "is powerfully mobilizing" (Valentino and Neuner 2016: 2). But they did not delve deeply into the theoretical ramifications of laws that were at once demobilizing and mobilizing. When juxtaposed with the phenomenon of backlash movements – where suppression is also mobilizing – it begins to seem that something more general is at work. Backlash movements are explosive and they are common. They encourage us to think again about elections.

The lessons can usefully go in both directions. A scholar of backlash movements might be tempted to pay attention only to the actions of the police and the reactions of protesters. But when we explored the effects of anger on voting and protesting back to back, new questions suggested themselves. For instance, when do elite actors (candidates, incumbents, organizers) try to stoke the anger of would-be participants, and what explains whether they succeed or fail? We hope that our research will stimulate more boundary-crossing of this kind.

THE DECISION OF WHOM TO VOTE FOR

Explanations of voters' party or candidate choice never became entangled in the problem of collective action; there has not been a "paradox of electoral choice," equivalent to the paradox of voting. The reason is that, once in the voting booth, the voter pays no additional cost in resources or time when she supports one candidate over another. Since no additional material costs are involved in voting for a preferred candidate, it seems natural to think that a person casts the ballot for the candidate whom she prefers. The citizen who wants the Social Democrats to win votes for the Social Democrats, because she wants them to win.

But things get more complicated when we move from *sincere* to *strategic* voting. Sincere voting means supporting one's most-favored candidate or party; strategic voting means casting one's ballot for the most preferred candidate who is likely to win. Now the idea of breaking a tie creeps back in. Cox (1997) explains the rationale behind strategic voting thus: "voting for the most palatable of the candidates *most likely to be tied* for first yields a higher expected utility than voting for" the most preferred candidate who is *unlikely* to be tied for first (Cox 1997: 75, emphasis added). The italicized passages bring to light a contradiction in the presumed expected utility approach of the strategic voter: rarely will one person's vote break a tie between the greater to the lesser of two evils. Recall that a distinct minority of citizens grossly overestimates the probability of a tie. Therefore, strategic voting cannot be explained as the unique rule that rational voters will use. Indeed, Duverger interpreted voters' distaste for "wasting" their votes as a "psychological factor" (1963[1954]: 224, 226).

Cox explained that strategic voting turns on what we are calling B calculations. The voter who sees a large utility differential in the victory of the likely winner over the first loser will vote strategically; those who see this differential as small compared to that between the likely first and second losers will vote sincerely. But if all of these calculations rely on the voter imagining himself breaking a tie, then a familiar question arises: Why should B come into the voter's calculations at all? At this point the lessons of our book become germane. If a person deviates from a course of action that, if taken by many, would produce a desired outcome, she is liable to experience dissonance, anxiety, and unhappiness. And she seems likely to experience these negative states to the degree that she sees much at stake in which candidate prevails. Just as there are costs of abstaining, there are likely to be *costs of defecting* from a course of action that is closely connected, in the polity at large, with one's desired outcome. Some people may experience these costs after a process of moral reflection. Others may be sensitive to the electoral choices of their friends and family members, who will hold them to account if they don't do the right thing. But our research strongly suggests that, for many, the dissonance entailed in costly defection will arise internally, out of their own cognitive and emotional processes.

Little wonder, then, that B-statements are so prevalent in campaigns, as we saw in Chapter 3. These statements do double-duty: they persuade supporters to turn out, and, in situations in which strategic voting may be called for, they frame the relative magnitude of B differentials between likely winners and first and second losers.

ELECTIONS AND PROTESTS AS INSTRUMENTS
OF DEMOCRACY

A final reflection is on the place of protests and elections in democracy. Ours is an era of skepticism about democracy. A long line of thinkers, beginning with eighteenth-century political philosophers, believed that officeholders who face repeated elections would be responsive to their constituents. But in the early years of the twenty-first century, many holes have been poked in this idea. Myopic voters let politicians off the hook for outcomes occurring early in their terms, at the same time that we reward or punish officeholders for events that may be trivial – whether the local sports team wins (e.g., Healy et al. 2010) – or over which governments have little control, such as floods or droughts. What's more, elections pack too many issues into a single decision (Achen and Bartels 2016). If democracy is not a mechanism of accountability, at least it may be an instantiation of political equality. Yet here, too, democratic practice deviates from theory. Democratic equality is belied by a long list of practices: vote suppression and vote buying; disenfranchisement of groups of citizens; legislative malapportionment and gerrymandering; and the influence of financially powerful actors and lobbies.

Democratic malaise goes beyond elections to less institutionalized forms of citizen action, including movements and protests. Reflecting on what he sees as the limp state of Western European democracy, Rosanvallon (2008) took it as a given that elections and parties are no longer trusted. For better or worse, we are in an era of "counterdemocracy," one symptom of which is frequent street movements. Counterdemocracy features critiques of government action rather than constructive politics.[3] A dimmer view of social movements still was taken by Shapiro (2016, chapter 3) and Przeworski (2017). Przeworski warned that "when conflicts spill to the streets, public support for authoritarian measures designed to maintain public order tends to increase, even if street protests are targeted precisely against authoritarian tendencies of governments" (2017: 31–2).

This is not the place to evaluate the factual bases of these dismal claims. There are reasons to doubt the most dire accounts of electoral democracy; that voters are myopic (for evidence against this, see, e.g., Aytaç 2018), pay attention to irrelevant events (e.g., Ashworth et al. 2018), or that money can always buy elections or public policy (Ansolabehere et al. 2003). It is hard to square this picture of the unaccountable president, prime minister, or legislator with officeholders who seem, if anything, too hemmed in by public opinion and too ready to pander. Nor do we believe that street protests inevitably push systems toward authoritarianism. The dynamics of protest and repression investigated in our book tell quite a different story, with protest leaders and police forces

---

[3] Rosanvallon may be too quick to push elections to the margins of democracy, as Schmitter (2010) contended.

having much to gain from restraining violence and paying heavy costs when they fail to do so. That they have incentives for restraint makes it unlikely that the picture painted by Przeworski is inevitable. History also offers several instances in which gross injustices were ignored by political party leaders and government officials and would have remained unaddressed had it not been for powerful social movements.

The two instruments of popular participation studied in this book complement each other in ways that can counteract democratic malaise. Where elections are blunt instruments because they pack so many issues into a single choice, protests offer clearer, more precise messages about what is on the public's mind. Where donors and lobbyists use financial resources to privately press legislators to do their bidding, protesters use widely distributed, yet valuable resources – above all, their time – to press governments toward preferred actions, and publicity is the name of their game. Where politicians may be tempted to pack unpopular measures into the early period of their terms, taking advantage of citizens' forgetfulness, protesters are reacting in real time to the actions and policies of governments.

On the other hand, protesters have no claim to represent the broader polity. Demonstrations are not spaces of equality so much as of passion and commitment. The population of protesters is always small, for reasons we have explained. Protests therefore fall short of elections in insuring that all who are affected by a collective decision can express their preferences about it – or about those who will make the decisions on their behalf. To the extent that many people absent themselves from electoral choices, elections, too, fall short of instantiating democratic equality. But in weighing how much we care about the outcome and how much inconvenience and risk we are willing to bear, many more citizens will participate at the polls than on the streets.

Despite the many stratagems used to drain elections of their equalizing qualities, they remain a great reckoning. Protests, with their focused message, their nimble timing, and their expression of passion and commitment, play a crucial role in democracies and in authoritarian settings. But it is elections that most powerfully institutionalize the fundamental democratic norm of political equality.

Bibliography

Abramowitz, Alan I. and Kyle L. Saunders. 2008. "Is Polarization a Myth?" *The Journal of Politics* 70(2): 542–55.

Abrams, Samuel, Torben Iversen, and David Soskice. 2010. "Informal Social Networks and Rational Voting." *British Journal of Political Science* 41(2): 229–57.

Acevedo, Bianca P., Elaine N. Aron, Arthur Aron, Matthew-Donald Sangster, Nancy Collins, and Lucy L. Brown. 2014. "The Highly Sensitive Brain: An fMRI Study of Sensory Processing Sensitivity and Response to Others' Emotions." *Brain and Behavior* 4(4): 580–94.

Acevedo, Melissa and Joachim I. Krueger. 2004. "Two Egocentric Sources of the Decision to Vote: The Voter's Illusion and the Belief in Personal Relevance." *Political Psychology* 25(1): 115–34.

Achen, Christopher H. and Larry M. Bartels. 2016. *Democracy for Realists: Why Elections Do Not Produce Responsive Government.* Princeton, NJ: Princeton University Press.

Adams, James, Jay Dow, and Samuel Merrill III. 2006. "The Political Consequences of Alienation-based and Indifference-based Voter Abstention: Applications to Presidential Elections." *Political Behavior* 28(1): 65–86.

Adams, James, and Samuel Merrill III. 2003. "Voter Turnout and Candidate Strategies in American Elections." *The Journal of Politics* 65(1): 161–89.

Aldrich, John H. 1993. "Rational Choice and Turnout." *American Journal of Political Science* 37(1): 246–78.

Ansolabehere, Stephen, John M. de Figueiredo, and James M. Snyder Jr. 2003. "Why is There So Little Money in U.S. Politics?" *Journal of Economic Perspectives* 17(1): 105–30.

Arcelus, Francisco and Allan H. Meltzer. 1975. "The Effect of Aggregate Economic Variables on Congressional Elections." *The American Political Science Review* 69(4): 1232–9.

Arceneaux, Kevin. 2012. "Cognitive Biases and the Strength of Political Arguments." *American Journal of Political Science* 56(2): 271–85.

Arceneaux, Kevin and David W. Nickerson. 2009. "Who is Mobilized to Vote? A Re-Analysis of 11 Field Experiments." *American Journal of Political Science* 53(1): 1–16.

Ashworth, Scott, Ethan Bueno de Mesquita, and Amanda Friedenberg. 2018. "Learning about Voter Rationality." *American Journal of Political Science* 62(1): 37–54.

Aytaç, Selim Erdem. 2018. "Relative Economic Performance and the Incumbent Vote: A Reference Point Theory." *The Journal of Politics* 80(1): 16–29.

Aytaç, S. Erdem, Eli Rau, and Susan Stokes. 2018. "Beyond Opportunity Costs: Campaign Messages, Anger, and Turnout among the Unemployed." Forthcoming, *British Journal of Political Science.*

Aytaç, S. Erdem, Luis Schiumerini, and Susan Stokes. 2017. "Protests and Repression in New Democracies." *Perspectives on Politics* 15(1): 62–82.

Aytaç, S. Erdem, Luis Schiumerini, and Susan Stokes. 2018. "Why Do People Join Backlash Protests? Lessons from Turkey." *Journal of Conflict Resolution* 62(6): 1205–28.

Baron, Reuben M. and David A. Kenny. 1986. "The Moderator–Mediator Variable Distinction in Social Psychological Research: Conceptual, Strategic, and Statistical Considerations." *Journal of Personality and Social Psychology* 51(6): 1173–82.

Barr, Robert R. 2009. "Populists, Outsiders, and Anti-Establishment Politics." *Party Politics* 15(1): 29–48.

Barry, Brian. 1970. *Sociologists, Economists, and Democracy.* Chicago, IL: The University of Chicago Press.

Beck, Nathaniel. 1975. "The Paradox of Minimax Regret." *The American Political Science Review* 69(3): 918.

Beissinger, Mark R. 2002. *Nationalist Mobilization and the Collapse of the Soviet State.* New York, NY: Cambridge University Press.

Beissinger, Mark R. 2013. "The Semblance of Democratic Revolution: Coalitions in Ukraine's Orange Revolution." *American Political Science Review* 107(3): 1–19.

Bendor, Jonathan, Daniel Diermeier, and Michael Ting. 2003. "A Behavioral Model of Turnout." *American Political Science Review* 97(2): 261–80.

Bennett, Lance W. and Alexandra Segerberg. 2013. *The Logic of Connective Action: Digital Media and the Personalization of Contentious Politics.* New York, NY: Cambridge University Press.

Berinsky, Adam J. and Gabriel S. Lenz. 2011. "Education and Political Participation: Exploring the Causal Link." *Political Behavior* 33(3): 357–73.

Berinsky, Adam J., Gregory A. Huber, Gabriel S. Lenz. 2012. "Evaluating Online Labor Markets for Experimental Research: Amazon.com's Mechanical Turk." *Political Analysis* 20(3): 351–68.

Berkowitz, Leonard, and Eddie Harmon-Jones. 2004. "Toward an Understanding of the Determinants of Anger." *Emotion* 4(2): 107–30.

Biggers, Daniel R., David J. Hendry, Alan S. Gerber, and Gregory A. Huber. 2017. "Experimental Evidence about Whether (and Why) Electoral Closeness Affects Turnout." Unpublished manuscript.

Blais, Andre. 2000. *To Vote or Not to Vote? The Merits and Limits Rational Choice Theory.* Pittsburgh, PA: University of Pittsburgh Press.

Blais, Andre. 2006. "What Affects Voter Turnout?" *Annual Review of Political Science* 9: 111–25.

Blais, Andre, and Robert Young. 1996. "Why Do People Vote? An Experiment in Rationality." Political Economy Research Group, University of Western Ontario.

Blais, Andre, Robert Young, and Miriam Lapp. 2000. "The Calculus of Voting: An Empirical Test." *European Journal of Political Research* 37(2): 181–201.

Blaydes, Lisa and James Lo. 2012. "One Man, One Vote, One Time? A Model of Democratization in the Middle East." *Journal of Theoretical Politics* 24(1): 110–46.

Brader, Ted. 2006. *Campaigning for Hearts and Minds: How Emotional Appeals in Political Ads Work*. Chicago, IL: The University of Chicago Press.

Brader, Ted, and George E. Marcus. 2013. "Emotion and Political Psychology." In *Oxford Handbook of Political Psychology*, Leonie Huddy, David O. Sears, and Jack S. Levy (Eds.) New York, NY: Oxford University Press, pp. 165–204.

Brennan, Geoffrey and Loren Lomasky. 1993. *Democracy and Decisions: The Pure Theory of Electoral Preference*. New York, NY: Cambridge University Press.

Brennan, Geoffrey and Loren E. Lomasky. 2000. "Is There a Duty to Vote?" *Social Philosophy and Policy* 17(1): 62–86.

Brody, Richard A. and Benjamin I. Page. 1973. "Indifference, Alienation, and Rational Decisions: The Effects of Candidate Evaluations on Turnout and the Vote." *Public Choice* 15: 1–17.

Bullock, John G., Donald P. Green, and Shang E. Ha. 2010. "Yes, but What's the Mechanism?(Don't Expect an Easy Answer)." *Journal of Personality and Social Psychology* 98(4): 550–8.

Bullock, John G., Alan S. Gerber, Seth J. Hill, and Gregory A. Huber. 2015. "Partisan Bias in Factual Beliefs about Politics." *Quarterly Journal of Political Science* 10(4): 519–78.

Burden, Barry C. and Amber Wichowsky. 2014. "Economic Discontent as a Mobilizer: Unemployment and Voter Turnout." *The Journal of Politics* 76(4): 887–98.

Butler, David, and Austin Ranney (Eds.) 1994. *Referendums Around the World: The Growing Use of Direct Democracy*. Washington, DC: American Enterprise Institute.

Campbell, A., Philip E. Converse, Warren E. Miller and Donald E. Stokes. 1960. *The American Voter*. New York, NY: John Wiley and Sons, Inc.

Carver, Charles S. 2004. "Negative Affects Deriving From the Behavioral Approach System." *Emotion* 4(1): 3–22.

Carver, Charles S. and Eddie Harmon-Jones. 2009. "Anger Is an Approach-Related Affect: Evidence and Implications." *Psychological Bulletin* 135(2): 183–204.

Castells, Manuel. 2012. *Networks of Outrage and Hope – Social Movements in the Internet Age*. Chichester, UK: Wiley.

Chen, Mengquin A. 2014. "Who Constructs My Identity? Understanding Turkish Youth in Gezi Protests." Unpublished manuscript, Princeton University, NJ.

Chenoweth, Erica and Jeremy Pressman. 2017. "This is What We Learned by Counting the Women's Marches." *The Washington Post*, February 7.

Chong, Dennis. 1991. *Collective Action and the Civil Rights Movement*. Chicago, IL: University of Chicago Press.

Citrin, Jack, Donald P. Green, and Morris Levy. 2014. "The Effects of Voter ID Notification on Voter Turnout: Results from a Large-Scale Field Experiment." *Election Law Journal* 13(2): 228–42.

Coate, Stephen and Michael Conlin. 2004. "A Group Rule: Utilitarian Approach to Voter Turnout: Theory and Evidence." *The American Economic Review* 94(5): 1476–504.

Conover, Pamela Johnston and Stanley Feldman. 1984. "How People Organize the Political World: A Schematic Model." *American Journal of Political Science* 28(1): 95–126.

Conover, Pamela Johnston and Stanley Feldman. 1986. "Emotional Reactions to the Economy: I'm Mad as Hell and I'm not Going to Take it Anymore." *American Journal of Political Science* 30(1): 50–78.

Coppock, Alexander. Forthcoming. "Generalizing from Survey Experiments Conducted on Mechanical Turk: A Replication Approach." *Political Science and Research Methods.*

Cox, Gary W. 1997. *Making Votes Count: Strategic Coordination in the World's Electoral Systems.* New York, NY: Cambridge University Press.

Cox, Gary W. and Michael C. Munger. 1989. "Closeness, Expenditures, and Turnout in the 1982 U.S. House Elections." *The American Political Science Review* 83(1): 217–31.

Crawford, John R. and Julie D. Henry. 2004. "The Positive and Negative Affect Schedule (PANAS): Construct Validity, Measurement Properties and Normative Data in a Large Non-Clinical Sample." *British Journal of Clinical Psychology* 43(3): 245–65.

Dahl, Robert A. 1989. *Democracy and Its Critics.* New Haven, CT: Yale University Press.

Dalton, Russell J. 2008. *Citizen Politics: Public Opinion and Political Parties in Advanced Industrial Democracies.* 5th Edition. Washington, DC: CQ Press.

Davenport, Christian. 2007. "State Repression and Political Order." *Annual Review of Political Science* 10(1): 1–23.

de Mesquita, Ethan Bueno. 2010. "Regime Change and Revolutionary Entrepreneurs." *American Political Science Review* 104(3): 446–66.

della Porta, Donatella. 2013. *Can Democracy be Saved? Participation, Deliberation, and Social Movements.* Malden, MA: Polity Press.

della Porta, Donatella and Sidney Tarrow. 2012. "Interactive Diffusion: The Coevolution of Police and Protest Behavior With an Application to Transnational Contention." *Comparative Political Studies* 45(1): 119–52.

Downs, Anthony. 1957. *An Economic Theory of Democracy.* New York, NY: Harper and Row.

Duverger, Maurice 1963[1954]. *Political Parties.* New York, NY: John Wiley and Sons.

El-Ghobashy, Mona. 2011. "The Praxis of the Egyptian Revolution." *Middle East Research and Information Project* 41(258): 2–13.

Enos, Ryan and Anthony Fowler. 2013. "Can Electoral Competition Mobilize Underrepresented Citizens? Evidence from a Field Experiment during a Tied Election." Unpublished manuscript.

Eres, Robert, Jean Decety, Winnifred R. Louis, and Pascal Molenberghs. 2015. "Individual Differences in Local Gray Matter Density Are Associated with Differences in Affective and Cognitive Empathy." *NeuroImage* 117: 305–10.

Fearon, James and David D. Laitin. 2003. "Ethnicity, Insurgency, and Civil War." *American Political Science Review* 97(1): 75–90.

Feather, Norman T. and Gordon E. O'Brien. 1986. "A Longitudinal Study of the Effects of Employment and Unemployment on School-Leavers." *Journal of Occupational Psychology* 59(2): 121–44.

Feddersen, Timothy J. 2004. "Rational Choice Theory and the Paradox of Not Voting." *Journal of Economic Perspectives* 18(1): 99–112.

Feddersen, Timothy and Alvaro Sandroni. 2006. "A Theory of Participation in Elections." *The American Economic Review* 96(4): 1271–82.

Ferejohn, John A. and Morris P. Fiorina. 1974. "The Paradox of Not Voting: A Decision Theoretic Analysis." *The American Political Science Review* 68(2): 525–36.

Ferejohn, John A. and Morris P. Fiorina. 1975. "Closeness Counts Only in Horseshoes and Dancing." *The American Political Science Review* 69(3): 920–5.

Finkel, Steven E., Edward N. Muller, and Karl-Dieter Opp. 1989. "Personal Influence, Collective Rationality, and Mass Political Action." *The American Political Science Review* 83(3): 885–903.

Fiorina, Morris P. 1978. "Economic Retrospective Voting in American National Elections: A Micro-Analysis." *American Journal of Political Science* 22(2): 426–43.

Fowler, James H. 2006. "Habitual Voting and Behavioral Turnout." *The Journal of Politics* 68(2): 335–44.

Francisco, Robert A. 1995. "The Relationship between Coercion and Protest: An Empirical Evaluation in Three Coercive States." *Journal of Conflict Resolution* 39(2): 263–82.

Francisco, Ronald. 2004. "After the Massacre: Mobilization in the Wake of Harsh Repression." *Mobilization: An International Quarterly* 9(2): 107–26.

Franco, Annie, Neil Malhotra, Gabor Simonovits, and L. J. Zigerell. 2017. "Developing Standards for Post-Hoc Weighting in Population-Based Survey Experiments." *Journal of Experimental Political Science* 4(2): 161–72.

Franklin, Mark N. 2004. *Voter Turnout and the Dynamics of Electoral Competition in Established Democracies Since 1945.* New York, NY: Cambridge University Press.

Franklin, Mark N. and Wolfgang P. Hirczy. 1998. "Separated Powers, Divided Government, and Turnout in U.S. Presidential Elections." *American Journal of Political Science* 42(1): 316–26.

Galais, Carol and Andre Blais. 2014a. "A Call of Duty in Hard Times: Duty to Vote and the Spanish Economic Crisis." *Research and Politics* 1(2): 1–8.

Galais, Carol and Andre Blais. 2014b. "Beyond Rationalization: Voting Out of Duty or Expressing Duty After Voting?" *International Political Science Review* 37(2): 213–99.

Gerber, Alan S., Donald P. Green, and Christopher W. Larimer. 2008. "Social Pressure and Voter Turnout: Evidence from a Large-Scale Field Experiment." *The American Political Science Review* 102(1): 33–48.

Gerber, Alan S., Donald P. Green, and Ron Shachar. 2003. "Voting May Be Habit-Forming: Evidence from a Randomized Field Experiment." *American Journal of Political Science* 47(3): 540–50.

Gerber, Alan S., Gregory A. Huber, David Dohert, Conor M. Dowling, and Nicole Schwartzberg. 2009. "Using Battleground States as a Natural Experiment to Test Theories of Voting." Unpublished manuscript.

Geschwender, James A. 1968. "Explorations in the Theory of Social Movements and Revolutions." *Social Forces* 47(2): 127–35.

Ginkel, John, and Alastair Smith. 1999. "So You Say You Want a Revolution: A Game Theoretic Explanation of Revolution in Repressive Regimes." *Journal of Conflict Resolution* 43(3): 291–316.

Goldstone, Jack A. 1998. "Social Movements or Revolutions?" In M. Giugni, Doug McAdam, and Charles Tilly (Eds.) *From Contention to Democracy*. New York, NY: Cambridge University Press.

Gonzalez-Barrera, Ana. 2017. "Mexican Lawful Immigrants Among the Least Likely to Become U.S.Citizens." Pew Research Center, June.

Granovetter, Mark. 1978. "Threshold Models of Collective Behavior." *American Journal of Sociology* 83(6): 1420–43.

Green, Donald P., and Ian Shapiro. 1994. *Pathologies of Rational Choice Theory: A Critique of Applications in Political Science*. New Haven, CT: Yale University Press.

Grimmer, Justin, Eitan Hersh, Marc Meredith, Jonathan Mummolo, and Clayton Nall. 2018. "Obstacles to Estimating Voter ID Laws' Effect on Turnout." *The Journal of Politics* 80(3): 1045–51.

Gupta, Devashree. 2017. *Protest Politics Today*. Medford, MA: Polity Press.

Gurr, Ted Robert. 1970. *Why Men Rebel*. Princeton, NJ: Princeton University Press.

Gusfield, Joseph. 1968. "Tradition and Modernity: Conflict and Congruence." *Journal of Social Issues* 24(4): 1–8.

Gusfield, Joseph. 1982. "Deviance in the Welfare State: The Alcoholism Profession and the Entitlements of Stigma." In M. Lewis (Ed.), *Research in Social Problems and Public Policy*. Greenwich, CT: JAI Press.

Hajnal, Zoltan, John Kuk, and Nazita Lajevardi. 2018. "We All Agree: Strict Voter ID Laws Disproportionately Burden Minorities." *Journal of Politics* 80(3): 1052–59.

Hajnal, Zoltan, Nazita Lajevardi, and Lindsay Nielson. 2017. "Voter Identification Laws and the Suppression of Minority Votes." *Journal of Politics* 79(2): 363–79.

Hakim, Danny, and Douglas Dalby. 2015. "Ireland Votes to Approve Gay Marriage, Putting Country in Vanguard." *The New York Times*, May 23.

Hamilton, V. Lee, William S. Hoffman, Clifford L. Broman, and David Rauma. 1993. "Unemployment, Distress, and Coping: A Panel Study of Autoworkers." *Journal of personality and social psychology* 65(2): 234–47.

Harsanyi, John C. 1977. "Morality and the Theory of Rational Behavior." *Social Research: An International Quarterly* 44(3): 623–56.

Harsanyi, John C. 1980. "Rule Utilitarianism, Rights, Obligations and The Theory of Rational Behavior." *Theory and Decision* 12: 115–33.

Healy, Andrew J. and Gabriel S. Lenz. 2014. "Substituting the End for the Whole: Why Voters Respond Primarily to the Election-Year Economy." *American Journal of Political Science* 58(1): 31–47.

Healy, Andrew J., Neil Malhotra, and Cecilia Hyunjung Mo. 2010. "Irrelevant Events Affect Voters' Evaluations of Government Performance." *Proceedings of the National Academy of Sciences* 107(29): 12804–9.

Highton, Benjamin. 2017. "Voter Identification Laws and Turnout in the United States." *Annual Review of Political Science* 20: 149–67.

Hirschman, Albert O. and Michael Rothschild. 1973. "The Changing Tolerance for Income inequality in the Course of Economic Development." *The Quarterly Journal of Economics* 87(4): 544–66.

Holbrook, Allyson L. and Jon A. Krosnick. 2010. "Social Desirability Bias in Voter Turnout Reports: Tests Using the Item Count Technique." *Public Opinion Quarterly* 74(1): 37–67.

Holmberg, Soren and Henrik Oscarsson. 2017. *Swedish Election Study 2010*. Swedish National Data Service. Version 1.0.

Huber, Gregory A., Seth J. Hill, and Gabriel S. Lenz. 2012. "Sources of Bias in Retrospective Decision Making: Experimental Evidence on Voters' Limitations in Controlling Incumbents." *American Political Science Review* 106(4): 720–41.

Huntington, Samuel P. 1968. *Political Order in Changing Societies*. New Haven, CT: Yale University Press.

Hutchings, Vincent L., Nicholas A. Valentino, Tasha S. Philpot, and Ismail K. White. 2006. "Racial Cues in Campaign News: The Effects of Candidate Strategies on Group Activation and Political Attentiveness among African Americans." In *Feeling Politics: Emotion in Political Information Processing*, David P. Redlawsk (Ed.) New York, NY: Palgrave, pp. 165–86.

Imai, Kosuke and Teppei Yamamoto. 2013. "Identification and Sensitivity Analysis for Multiple Causal Mechanisms: Revisiting Evidence from Framing Experiments." *Political Analysis* 21(2): 141–71.

Imai, Kosuke, Luke Keele, Dustin Tingley, and Teppei Yamamoto. 2011. "Unpacking the Black Box of Causality: Learning about Causal Mechanisms from Experimental and Observational Studies." *American Political Science Review* 105(4): 765–89.

Incantalupo, Matthew B. 2011. "The Effects of Unemployment on Voter Turnout in U.S. National Elections." Unpublished manuscript.

Iyer, Aarti, Toni Schmader, and Brian Lickel. 2007. "Individuals Protest the Perceived Transgressions of Their Country: The Role of Anger, Shame, and Guilt." *Personality and Social Psychology Bulletin* 33(4): 572–87.

Jackman, Robert W. 1987. "Political Institutions and Voter Turnout in the Industrial Democracies." *The American Political Science Review* 81(2): 405–24.

Jasper, James M. 1998. "The Emotions of Protest: Affective and Reactive Emotions in and around Social Movements." *Sociological Forum* 13(3): 397–424.

Jasper, James M. 2011. "Emotions and Social Movements: Twenty Years of Theory and Research." *Annual Review of Sociology* 37: 14.1–14.19.

Jasper, James M. 2014. "Constructing Indignation: Anger Dynamics in Protest Movements." *Emotion Review* 6(3): 208–13.

Jenkins, J. Craig. 1983. "Resource Mobilization Theory and the Study of Social Movements." *Annual Review of Sociology* 9: 527–53.

Kalyvas, Stathis. 2006. *The Logic of Violence in Civil War*. New York, NY: Cambridge University Press.

Kanazawa, Satoshi. 1998. "A Possible Solution to the Paradox of Voter Turnout." *The Journal of Politics* 60(4): 974–95.

Karlan, Pamela S. 1994. "Not by Money but by Virtue Won? Vote Trafficking and the Voting Rights System." *Virginal Law Review* 80(7): 1455–75.

Kasara, Kimuli and Pavithra Suryanarayan. 2015. "When do the Rich Vote Less Than the Poor and Why? Explaining Turnout Inequality Across the World." *American Journal of Political Science* 59(3): 613–27.

King, Gary, Matthew Knowles, and Steven Melendez. 2010. "ReadMe: Software for Automated Content Analysis." Available at: https://gking.harvard.edu/readme

King, Gary, Jennifer Pan, and Margaret E. Roberts. 2013. "How Censorship in China Allows Government Criticism but Silences Collective Expression." *American Political Science Review* 107(2): 1–18.

King, Gary, Jennifer Pan, and Margaret E. Roberts. 2014. "Reverse Engineering Chinese Censorship through Randomized Experimentation and Participant Observation." *Science* 6199(345): 1–10.

King, Gary, Jennifer Pan, and Margaret E. Roberts. 2017. "How the Chinese Government Fabricates Social Media Posts for Strategic Distraction, not Engaged Argument." *American Political Science Review* 111(3): 484–501.

Klandermans, Bert. 1984. "Mobilization and Participation: Social-Psychological Expansions of Resource Mobilization Theory." *American Sociological Review* 49(5): 583–600.

Klandermans, Bert and Dirk Oegema. 1987. "Potentials, Networks, Motivations, and Barriers: Steps Towards Participation in Social Movements." *American Sociological Review* 52(4): 519–31.

Kolodny, Niko. 2014. "Rule Over None I: What Justifies Democracy?" *Philosophy and Public Affairs* 42(3): 195–229.

Konda. 2013. *Gezi Park Survey: Who Is Involved, What Do They Want, and Why Are They There?* Istanbul: Konda Research and Consultancy.

Konda. 2014. *Gezi Report: Public Perceptions of the 'Gezi Protests,' Who Were the People at Gezi Park?* Istanbul: Konda Research and Consultancy.

Kornhauser, William. 1959. *The Politics of Mass Society.* Glencoe, IL: The Free Press.

Krueger, Alan B., and Andreas I. Mueller. 2012. "The Lot of the Unemployed: A Time Use Perspective." *Journal of the European Economic Association* 10(4): 765–94.

Kuklinski, James H., Robert C. Luskin, and John Bolland. 1991. "Where is the Schema? Going Beyond the 'S' Word in Political Psychology." *American Political Science Review* 85(4): 1341–80.

Kuran, Timur. 1990. "Private and Public Preferences." *Economics and Philosophy* 6(1): 1–26.

Kuran, Timur. 1991. "Now Out of Never: The Element of Surprise in the East European Revolution of 1989." *World Politics* 44(1): 7–48.

Kuran, Timur. 1995. *Private Truths, Public Lies: The Social Consequences of Preference Falsification.* Cambridge, MA: Cambridge University Press.

Kuran, Timur and Diego Romero. 2018. "The Logic of Revolutions: Rational Choice Perspectives." *Oxford Handbook of Public Choice* (Vol. 2), Ch. 18. Oxford: Oxford University Press.

Larsen, R. J., E. Diener, and R. Lucas. 2002. "Emotion: Models, Measures, and Individual Differences." In *Emotions At Work*, R. Lord, R. Klimoski, and R. Kanfer (Eds.) San Francisco, CA: Jossey-Bass, pp. 64–106.

Lawrence, Adria K. 2017. "Repression and Activism among the Arab Spring's First Movers: Evidence from Morocco's February 20th Movement." *British Journal of Political Science* 47(3): 699–718.

Lazarus, Richard S. 1991. "Emotion and Adaptation." New York, NY: Oxford University Press.

Le Bon, Gustave. [1895] 1960. *The Crowd: A Study of the Popular Mind* (translation of Psychologie des Foules). New York, NY: Viking Press.

LeDuc, Lawrence. 2015. "Referendums and Deliberative Democracy." *Electoral Studies* 38: 139–48.

Ledyard, John O. 1984. "The Pure Theory of Large Two-Candidate Elections." *Public Choice* 44(1): 7–41.

Leighley, Jan E. and Jonathan Nagler. 2014. *Who Votes Now? Demographics, Issues, Inequality, and Turnout in the United States.* Princeton, NY: Princeton University Press.

Lerner, Jennifer and Dacher Keltner. 2001. "Fear, Anger, and Risk." *Journal of Personality and Social Psychology* 81(1): 146–59.

Linn, Margaret W., Richard Sandifer, and Shayna Stein. 1985. "Effects of Unemployment on Mental and Physical Health." *American Journal of Public Health* 75(5): 502–6.

Lohmann, Susanne. 1994. "The Dynamics of Informational Cascades: The Monday Demonstrations in Leipzig, East Germany, 1989–91." *World Politics* 47(October): 42–101.

MacKuen, Michael, Jennifer Wolak, Luke Keele, and George E. Marcus. 2010. "Civic Engagements: Resolute Partisanship or Reflective Deliberation." *American Journal of Political Science* 54(2): 440–58.

Marcus, George E., Michael MacKuen, and W. Russell Neuman. 2000. *Affective Intellingence and Political Judgment.* Chicago, IL: The University of Chicago Press.

McAdam, Doug. 1986. "Recruitment to High-Risk Activism: The Case of Freedom Summer." *American Journal of Sociology* 92(1): 64–90.

McAdam, Doug. 1995. "'Initiator' and 'Spin-off' Movements: Diffusion Processes in Protest Cycles." In *Repertoires and Cycles of Collective Action*, edited by Mark Traugott, 217–40. Durham, NC: Duke University Press.

McAdam, Doug. 1999. *Political Process and the Development of Black Insurgency, 1930–1970.* 2nd Edition. Chicago, IL: The University of Chicago Press.

McCarthy, John D. and Mayer N. Zald. 1973. *The Trend of Social Movements in America: Professionalization and Resource Mobilization.* Morristown, NJ: General Learning Press.

McCarthy, John D. and Mayer N. Zald. 1977. "Resource Mobilization and Social Movements: A Partial Theory." *The American Journal of Sociology* 82(6): 1212–41.

McDonald, Karl. 2015. "Ireland's Same-sex Marriage Vote: Irish Living in UK Flock Back to Make Referendum." *The Independent*, May 2015.

Medina, Luis Fernando. 2007. *A Unified Theory of Collective Action and Social Change.* Ann Arbor, MI: The University of Michigan Press.

Medina, Luis Fernando. 2018. *Beyond the Turnout Paradox: The Political Economy of Electoral Participation.* Cham, Switzerland: Springer.

Melo, Daniela F. and Daniel Stockemer. 2014. "Age and Political Participation in Germany, France and the UK: A Comparative Analysis." *Comparative European Politics* 12(1): 33–53.

Miller, Kevin W., Wilder, Lora B., Stillman, Frances A., and Becker, Diane M. 1997. "The feasibility of a street-intercept survey method in an African-American community." *American Journal of Public Health* 87(4): 655–8.

Morton, Rebecca B. 1987. "A Group Majority Voting Model of Public Good Provision." *Social Choice and Welfare* 4(2): 117–31.

Morton, Rebecca B. 1991. "Groups in Rational Turnout Models." *American Journal of Political Science* 35(3): 758–76.

Mutz, Diana C. 2002. "The Consequences of Cross-Cutting Networks for Political Participation." *American Journal of Political Science* 46(4): 838–55.

Niemi, Richard. 1976. "Costs of Voting and Nonvoting." *Public Choice* 27(1): 115–19.

Oberschall, Anthony. 1973. *Social Conflict and Social Movements*. Englewood Cliffs, NJ: Prentice-Hall.

Oberschall, Anthony. 1978. "Theories of Social Conflict." *Annual Review of Sociology* 4: 291–315.

Ojeda, Christopher. 2015. "Depression and political participation." *Social Science Quarterly* 96(5): 1226–43.

Opp, Karl-Dieter. 1991. "Process of Collective Political Action: A Dynamic Model and the Results of a Computer Simulation." *Rationality and Society* 3(2): 215–51.

Opp, Karl-Dieter. 1994. "Repression and Revolutionary Action: East Germany in 1989." *Rationality and Society* 6(1): 101–38.

Opp, Karl-Dieter and Wolfgang Roehl. 1990. "Repression, Micromobilization, and Political Protest." *Social Forces* 69(2): 521–47.

Orum, Anthony. 1972. *Black Students in Protest: A Study of the Origins of the Black Student Movement*. Arnold M. and Caroline Rose Monograph Series. Washington, DC: American Sociological Association.

Palfrey, Thomas R. and Howard Rosenthal. 1983. "A Strategic Calculus of Voting." *Public Choice* 41(1): 7–53.

Palfrey, Thomas R. and Howard Rosenthal. 1985. "Voter Participation and Strategic Uncertainty." *The American Political Science Review* 79(1): 62–78.

Pearlman, Wendy. 2013. "Emotions and the Microfoundations of the Arab Uprisings." *Perspectives on Politics* 11(2): 387–409.

Pedersen, Roger D. 2002. *Understanding Ethnic Violence: Fear, Hatred, and Resentment in Twentieth-Century Eastern Europe*. New York, NY: Cambridge University Press.

Pierskalla, Jan Henryk. 2010. "Protest, Deterrence, and Escalation: The Strategic Calculus of Government Repression." *Journal of Conflict Resolution* 54(1): 117–45.

Plane, Dennis L., and Joseph Gershtenson. 2004. "Candidates' Ideological Locations, Abstention, and Turnout in U.S. Midterm Senate Elections." *Political Behavior* 26(1): 69–93.

Pogash, Carol. 2016. "Unsettling U.S. Political Climate Galvanizes Muslims to Vote." *The New York Times*, June 1.

Powell, G. Bingham. 1982. *Contemporary Democracies: Participation, Stability, and Violence*. Cambridge, MA: Harvard University Press.

Price, Richard H., Jin Nam Choi, and Amiram D. Vinokur. 2002 "Links in the Chain of Adversity following Job Loss: How Financial Strain and Loss of Personal Control lead to Depression, Impaired Functioning, and Poor Health." *Journal of Occupational Health Psychology* 7(4): 302–12.

Przeworski, Adam. 1991. *Democracy and the Market: Political and Economic Reforms in Eastern Europe and Latin America*. New York, NY: Cambridge University Press.

Przeworski, Adam. 2009. "Conquered or Granted? A History of Suffrage Extensions." *British Journal of Political Science* 39(2): 291–321.

Przeworski, Adam. 2017. "What's Happening?" Unpublished manuscript.

Quattrone, George A. and Amos Tversky. 1984. "Causal Versus Diagnostic Contingencies: On Self-Deception and on the Voter's Illusion." *Journal of Personality and Social Psychology* 46(2): 237–48.

Quattrone, George A. and Amos Tversky. 1988. "Contrasting Rational and Psychological Analyses of Political Choice." *The American Political Science Review* 82(3): 719–36.

Qvortrup, Matt. 2013. *Direct Democracy: A Comparative Study of the Theory and Practice of Government by the People.* Manchester: Manchester University Press.

Riker, William H. and Peter C. Ordeshook. 1968. "A Theory of the Calculus of Voting." *The American Political Science Review* 62(1): 25–42.

Rolfe, Meredith. 2012. *Voter Turnout: A Social Theory of Political Participation.* New York, NY: Cambridge University Press.

Rosanvallon, Pierre. 2008. *Counter-Democracy: Politics in an Age of Distrust.* New York, NY: Cambridge University Press.

Rosenstone, Steven J. 1982. "Economic Adversity and Voter Turnout." *American Journal of Political Science* 26(1): 25–46.

Rosenstone, Steven J. and John Mark Hansen. 1993. *Mobilization, Participation, and Democracy in America.* New York, NY: Macmillan Publishing Company.

Samuels, David J. and Cesar Zucco. 2013. "Using Facebook as a Subject Recruitment Tool for Survey-Experimental Research." Working paper available at SSRN: https://ssrn.com/abstract=2101458 or http://dx.doi.org/10.2139/ssrn.2101458

Samuels, David J., and Cesar Zucco. 2014. "The Power of Partisanship in Brazil: Evidence from Survey Experiments." *American Journal of Political Science* 58(1): 212–25.

Schmitter, Philippe C. 2010. "Democracy and Distrust: A Discussion of Counter-Democracy: Politics in an Age of Distrust." *Perspectives on Politics* 8(3): 887–89.

Schuessler, Alexander A. 2000a. *A Logic of Expressive Choice.* Princeton, NJ: Princeton University Press.

Schuessler, Alexander A. 2000b. "Expressive Voting." *Rationality and Society* 12(1): 87–119.

Schwartz, Michael. 1976. *Radical Protest and Social Structure: The Southern Farmers' Alliance and Cotton Tenancy, 1880–1890.* Chicago, IL: The University of Chicago Press.

Schwartz, Thomas. 1987. "Your Vote Counts on Account of the Way It is Counted: An Institutional Solution to the Paradox of Not Voting." *Public Choice* 54(2): 101–21.

Shachar, Ron and Barry Nalebuff. 1999. "Follow the Leader: Theory and Evidence on Political Participation." *American Economic Review* 89(3): 525–47.

Shadmehr, Mehdi, and Raphael Boleslavsky. 2015. "Repression and the Spread of Protest." Unpublished manuscript.

Shapiro, Ian. 2016. *Politics against Domination.* Cambridge, MA: Harvard Belknap.

Shaw, Daron R. 2006. *The Race to 270: The Electoral College and the Campaign Strategies of 2000 and 2004.* Chicago, IL: University of Chicago Press.

Siegel, David A. 2011. "When Does Repression Work? Collective Action in Social Networks." *The Journal of Politics* 73(4): 993–1010.

Sinclair, Betsy. 2012. *The Social Citizen.* Chicago, IL: University of Chicago Press.

Smelser, Neil J. 1968. *Essays in Sociological Explanation.* Englewood Cliffs, NJ: Prentice Hall.

Sondheimer, Rachel Milstein and Donald P. Green. 2010. "Using Experiments to Estimate the Effects of Education on Voter Turnout." *American Journal of Political Science* 54(1): 174–89.

Steiner, Peter M., Christiane Atzmuller, and Dan Su. 2016. "Designing Valid and Reliable Vignette Experiments for Survey Research: A Case Study on the Fair Gender Income Gap." *Journal of Methods and Measurement in the Social Sciences* 7(2): 52–94.

Stephens, Stephen V. 1975. "The Paradox of Not Voting: Comment." *American Political Science Review* 69(3): 914–915.

Stokes, Susan C., Thad Dunning, Marcelo Nazareno, and Valeria Brusco. 2013. *Brokers, Voters, and Clientelism: The Puzzle of Distributive Politics.* New York, NY: Cambridge University Press.

Tarrow, Sidney G. [1994] 2011. *Power in Movement: Social Movements and Contentious Politics.* New York, NY: Cambridge University Press.

Tavits, Margit. 2009. "Direct Presidential Elections and Turnout in Parliamentary Contests." *Political Research Quarterly* 62(1): 42–54.

Terracciano, Antonio, Robert R. McCrae, and Paul T. Costa. 2003. "Factorial and Construct Validity of the Italian Positive and Negative Affect Schedule (PANAS)." *European Journal of Psychological Assessment* 19(2): 131–41.

Tezcür, Güneş Murat. 2016. "Ordinary People, Extraordinary Risks: Participation in an Ethnic Rebellion." *American Political Science Review* 110(2): 247–64.

Thalheimer, Kim. 1995. "The Impact of the Probability Factor on the Decision to Vote." Unpublished manuscript.

Thomas, Emma F., Craig McGarty and Kenneth I. Mavor. 2009. "Transforming 'Apathy into Movement:' The Role of Prosocial Emotions in Motivating Action for Social Change." *Personality and Social Psychology Review* 13(4): 310–33.

Tilly, Charles. 1973. "Does Modernization Breed Revolution?" *Comparative Politics* 5(3): 425–47.

Trejo, Guillermo. 2014. "The Ballot and the Street: An Electoral Theory of Social Protest in Autocracies." *Perspectives on Politics* 12(2): 332–52.

Uhlaner, Carol J. 1989. "Relational Goods and Participation: Incorporating Sociability into a Theory of Rational Action." *Public Choice* 62: 253–85.

Valentino, Nicholas A., Ted Brader, Eric W. Groenendyk, Krysha Gregorowicz, and Vincent L. Hutchings. 2011. "Election Night's Alright for Fighting: The Role of Emotions in Political Participation." *The Journal of Politics* 73(1): 156–70.

Valentino, Nicholas A., Krysha Gregorowicz, and Eric W. Groenendyk. 2009. "Efficacy, Emotions, and the Habit of Participation." *Political Behavior* 31(3): 307–30.

Valentino, Nicholas A. and Fabian G. Nuener. 2016. "Why the Sky Didn't Fall: Mobilizing Anger in Reaction to Voter ID Laws." *Political Psychology* 20(20): 1–20.

Van Stekelenburg, Jacquelien and Bert Klandermans. 2013. "The Social Psychology of Protest." *Current Sociology Review* 61(5–6): 886–905.

Van Stekelenburg, Jacquelien, Dirk Oegema, and Bert Klandermans. 2010. "No Radicalization Without Identification: Dynamics of Radicalization and Polarization

Within and Between Two Opposing Web Forums." In A. Azzi, X. Chryssochoou and B. Klandermans (Eds.) *Identity and Participation in Culturally Diverse Societies: A Multidisciplinary Perspective*, Ch. 13. Oxford: Blackwell Wiley.

Van Zomeren, Martijn. 2013. "Four Core Social-Psychological Motivations to Undertake Collective Action." *Social and Personality Psychology Compass* 7(6): 378–88.

Van Zomeren, Martijn, Tom Postmes, and Russell Spears. 2008. "Toward an Integrative Social Identity Model of Collective Action: A Quantitative Research Synthesis of Three Socio-Psychological Perspectives." *Psychological Bulletin* 134(4): 504–35.

Vavreck, Lynn. 2009. *The Message Matters: The Economy and Presidential Campaigns*. Princeton, NJ: Princeton University Press.

Verba, Sidney, Kay Lehman Schlozman and Henry E. Brady. 1995. *Voice and Equality: Civic Voluntarism in American Politics*. New York, NY: Cambridge University Press.

Waismel-Manor, Israel, Gal Ifergane, and Hagit Cohen. 2011. "When Endocrinology and Democracy Collide: Emotions, Cortisol and Voting at National Elections." *European Neuropsychopharmacology* 21(11): 789–95.

Walder, Andrew G. 2009. "Political Sociology and Social Movements." *Annual Review of Sociology* 35: 393–412.

Walker, Shaun. 2013. "Ukraine Protests: Outrage as Police Attack Kiev Barricades." *The Guardian*, December 11.

Wasow, Omar. 2016. "Do Protest Tactics Matter? Evidence from the 1960s Black Insurgency." Paper presented at the Race, Ethnicity, and Immigration Colloquium, University of California, Berkeley, CA, February 9, 2016.

Watson, David, Lee Anna Clark, and Auke Tellegen. 1988. "Development and Validation of Brief Measures of Positive and Negative Affect: The PANAS Scales." *Journal of Personality and Social Psychology* 54(6): 1063–70.

Whiteley, Paul, Harold D. Clarke, David Sanders and Marianne Stewart. 2013. *Affluence, Austerity and Electoral Change in Britain*. New York, NY: Cambridge University Press.

Whiteley, Paul, and David Sanders. 2014. British Election Study, 2010: Face-to-Face Survey [computer file]. Colchester, Essex: UK Data Archive [distributor].

Wilson, John. 1973. *Introduction to Social Movements*. New York, NY: Basic Books.

Wiltfang, Gregory L. and Doug McAdam. 1991. "The Costs and Risks of Social Activism: A Study of Sanctuary Movement Activism." *Social Forces* 69(4): 987–1010.

Wolfinger, Raymond E. and Steven J. Rosenstone. 1980. *Who Votes?* New Haven, CT: Yale University Press.

Wood, Elisabeth Jean. 2003. *Insurgent Collective Action and Civil War in El Salvador*. New York, NY: Cambridge University Press.

Zipp, John F. 1985. "Perceived Representativeness and Voting: An Assessment of the Impact of 'Choice' vs. 'Echoes'." *American Political Science Review* 79(1): 50–61.

Index

Other Books in the Series (continued from page ii)

Maria Victoria Murillo, *Labor Unions, Partisan Coalitions, and Market Reforms in Latin America*

Monika Nalepa, *Skeletons in the Closet: Transitional Justice in Post-Communist Europe*

Noah L. Nathan, *Electoral Politics and Africa's Urban Transition: Class and Ethnicity in Ghana*

Ton Notermans, *Money, Markets, and the State: Social Democratic Economic Policies since 1918*

Simeon Nichter, *Votes for Survival: Relational Clientelism in Latin America*

Aníbal Pérez-Liñán, *Presidential Impeachment and the New Political Instability in Latin America*

Roger D. Petersen, *Understanding Ethnic Violence: Fear, Hatred, and Resentment in 20th Century Eastern Europe*

Roger D. Petersen, *Western Intervention in the Balkans: The Strategic Use of Emotion in Conflict*

Simona Piattoni, ed., *Clientelism, Interests, and Democratic Representation*

Paul Pierson, *Dismantling the Welfare State?: Reagan, Thatcher, and the Politics of Retrenchment*

Marino Regini, *Uncertain Boundaries: The Social and Political Construction of European Economies*

Kenneth M. Roberts, *Changing Course in Latin America: Party Systems in the Neoliberal Era*

Marc Howard Ross, *Cultural Contestation in Ethnic Conflict*

Anria Santiago, *When Movements Become Parties*

Roger Schoenman, *Networks and Institutions in Europe's Emerging Markets*

Ben Ross Schneider, *Hierarchical Capitalism in Latin America: Business, Labor, and the Challenges of Equitable Development*

Lyle Scruggs, *Sustaining Abundance: Environmental Performance in Industrial Democracies*

Jefferey M. Sellers, *Governing from Below: Urban Regions and the Global Economy*

Yossi Shain and Juan Linz, eds., *Interim Governments and Democratic Transitions*

Beverly Silver, *Forces of Labor: Workers' Movements and Globalization since 1870*

Theda Skocpol, *Social Revolutions in the Modern World*

Prerna Singh, *How Solidarity Works for Welfare: Subnationalism and Social Development in India*

Austin Smith et al, *Selected Works of Michael Wallerstein*

Regina Smyth, *Candidate Strategies and Electoral Competition in the Russian Federation: Democracy Without Foundation*

Richard Snyder, *Politics after Neoliberalism: Reregulation in Mexico*

David Stark and László Bruszt, *Postsocialist Pathways: Transforming Politics and Property in East Central Europe*

Sven Steinmo, *The Evolution of Modern States: Sweden, Japan, and the United States*

Sven Steinmo, Kathleen Thelen, and Frank Longstreth, eds., *Structuring Politics: Historical Institutionalism in Comparative Analysis*